Praise for *Think Like a Rock Star*

"Mack Collier knows the simple but powerful truth: in the social economy, your ability to acquire new customers will depend on your ability to delight your current customers and convert them into passionate fans of your brand. He shows you why; he shows you how; he inspires you to think like a rock star. Buy this book! Stop managing campaigns and start building movements!"

—EKATERINA WALTER, Social Innovator at Intel and
bestselling author of *Think Like Zuck: The Five Business Secrets
of Facebook's Improbably Brilliant CEO Mark Zuckerberg*

"You thought that rock stars and business successes focus only on themselves. Nothing could be further from the truth. The real success stories come from people who focus on others. To lead is to serve, and to serve effectively, you need to know your customers. Mack Collier gets that and highlights it well in this book."

—SCOTT MONTY, Global Head of Social Media at Ford Motor Company

"'Preparing for the Zombie Apocalypse' is a brilliant mock-awareness campaign produced by the CDC that earned 30,000 views on the first day it was published. Mack Collier shares insights from case studies such as this, showing how even conservative brands can create YouTube sensations, while humanizing the brand along the way. I've applied this type of approach on social campaigns at IBM and Cisco, and know firsthand that any brand can learn a great deal from these lessons."

—TIM WASHER, Senior Marketing Manager of Social Media at Cisco

"If you're ready to take the plunge and commit yourself to building a better business, together with your customers, then *Think Like a Rock Star* is your guidebook to achieving it! Simple, jargon-fr[...]
authentic style, this book explains exactly why[...]
customers, and how you can turn your most [...]
brand advocates. Mack delivers his passion f[...]

D1506347

of customer-centric marketing, and in-depth understanding of what makes the most devoted of fans tick in language we can all relate to.

"Fun to read, *Think Like a Rock Star* is guaranteed to give you numerous a-ha! moments that will inspire you to do better. By the end of this book, you'll be thinking of marketing and engagement strategies from the viewpoint of a fan, and you'll know what you need to do to connect with them.

"I love this book for many reasons, but most of all because for every 'why,' there is a 'how'! The case studies, tips, and social media advice are perfectly aligned with Mack's underlying mission of helping brands understand the true value of their most passionate customers. It's a must read for modern-day marketers! I highly recommend you purchase multiple copies: one for you and one for each member of your team."

—KELLY HUNGERFORD, Community Manager at Paper.Li

THINK LIKE A
ROCK STAR

HOW TO CREATE
SOCIAL MEDIA AND **MARKETING**
STRATEGIES THAT
TURN CUSTOMERS INTO FANS

MACK COLLIER

FOREWORD BY KATHY SIERRA

Mc
Graw
Hill
Education

New York   Chicago   San Francisco   Lisbon   London   Madrid   Mexico City
Milan   New Delhi   San Juan   Seoul   Singapore   Sydney   Toronto

Copyright © 2013 by Mack Collier. All rights reserved. Printed in the United States of America. Except as permitted under the United States Copyright Act of 1976, no part of this publication may be reproduced or distributed in any form or by any means, or stored in a data base or retrieval system, without prior written permission of the publisher.

1 2 3 4 5 6 7 8 9 0   DOC/DOC   1 9 8 7 6 5 4 3

ISBN: 978-0-07-180609-1
MHID: 0-07-180609-1

e-ISBN: 978-0-07-180610-7
e-MHID: 0-07-180610-5

McGraw-Hill books are available at special quantity discounts to use as premiums and sales promotions, or for use in corporate training programs. To contact a representative, please e-mail us at bulksales@mcgraw-hill.com.

This book is printed on acid-free paper.

★

To Mary Camron—

When I was a child,

you once made me a cape and

helped me believe I could fly

★

CONTENTS

———

Foreword   ix

Preface   xi

Introduction   1

PART 1

THE FOUR REASONS
ROCK STARS HAVE FANS
(AND YOUR COMPANY
HAS CUSTOMERS)

———

1 ★ Rock Stars Are Fans Themselves   15

2 ★ Rock Stars Look for Ways to Shift Control to Their Fans   31

3 ★ Rock Stars Find the Bigger Idea Behind the Music   47
They Create

4 ★ Rock Stars Embrace and Empower Their Fans   67

PART 2

UNDERSTANDING AND CONNECTING WITH YOUR FANS

5 ★ Who Your Fans Are and How You Can Connect with Them   89

6 ★ How to Handle Negative Comments and Convert   107
Angry Customers Into Passionate Fans

PART 3

BUILDING A FAN-CENTRIC COMPANY

7 ★ How to Organize Your Employees So They Can   127
Better Connect with Your Customers

8 ★ How to Organize and Mobilize Your   143
Customer and Brand Advocates

9 ★ How to Empower Your Fans and Employees   159

10 ★ How to Help Your Brand Ambassadors   171
Connect with Your Customers

11 ★ What Comes Next   183

Appendix   189

Acknowledgments   196

Index   198

Foreword

For nearly a decade, I've publicly and gleefully criticized social media marketing and its proponents. Imagine my surprise when I was asked to write a foreword for *this* book. That tells you something about Mack Collier.

While brands relentlessly exploit social media for the purpose of *manipulating* customers, Mack relentlessly pushes us toward a different, deeper, more sustainable vision of using social media to *empower* customers. However, this is not *just* a vision; it's a practical, well-tested approach used by... rock stars. Actual rock stars. With actual fans. Mack has spent years learning from—and applying the lessons of—the way rock stars ignite a passionate, engaged fan base.

He looked for both inspiration and techniques among the one group that has *always* known what most brands don't: people don't become fans of a brand because they like the *brand*. They become fans of the brand because they like *themselves*. Rock stars know that it's not *really* about them. It's about what they inspire and enable in their fans.

This might seem counterintuitive. Aren't rock stars the *ultimate* examples of "it's all about *me*"? But as Mack shows us over and over, the most successful rock stars are those who have acted as tools

Difference between Brands and Rockstars

of change for their fans. Rock stars aren't just making better fans; they're making their fans better. More connected. More interesting. More alive. And this cannot be faked. Mack Collier understands how rock stars empower their fans in a way that's meaningful to those fans, and he helps us enrich the lives of *our* fans. *That's* why I love this book.

—KATHY SIERRA

Preface

Allow me, if you will, to turn back the clock to 1990 for a minute. Mrs. Smith has just eaten at your brand's restaurant with her family. In 1990, whether Mrs. Smith's experience at your restaurant was particularly wonderful or particularly horrid, her ability to communicate with others about that experience was severely limited by the technology that was available to her. Mrs. Smith probably doesn't have Internet access, and even if she does, most of her friends probably don't. So her best bet when it comes to communicating with others about her experience with your brand is probably the landline telephone in her home. This means that the only people who are likely to hear about Mrs. Smith's experience (good or bad) are her friends who live in the same area. That's probably not a very large group, and in any event, your brand wouldn't be likely to know about Mrs. Smith's experience unless she communicated with your brand directly. Her feedback was trapped in a mostly analog world where your brand couldn't access it.

Then we have rock stars. Rock stars have always had fans, even when the technology that was available to them didn't lend itself to facilitating a direct connection between them and their fans. So how did rock stars get over the technological hurdles in years past? In large part, it was through live performances.

If you were an aspiring rock star in 1990, how would you launch your career? You would probably find places to play locally, bars or clubs in your area. It's quite possible that only a few people would come to hear you play, but you would have the ability to connect directly with those people. If you were just starting out, you might play at a local bar for an audience of 10 to 20 people, then collect $50 from the bar's owner (which you probably would then spend on drinks with the people who had attended your performance). So at the beginning of your music career, you would be connecting directly with the people who had an interest in your music. Over time, if you had a knack for creating and performing good music, you'd probably play for larger crowds, and eventually you might even be lucky enough to sign a record deal. But from the start, even when the technology didn't make the process easy, you found a way to connect directly with your fans.

This is a big reason why rock stars have always had fans: because they have always had ways of connecting with them directly. Not only have rock stars always understood the value of connecting directly with their customers and cultivating fans, but they have *wanted* to be close to their fans. Rock stars *thrive* on having a close connection with their fans.

In this day and age, people have the technologies in place to quickly and easily create and share content about rock stars—and brands. And it's no surprise that many rock stars are utilizing social media marketing as a new channel for doing something that they have always done successfully: connecting directly with their fans. But the problem for brands is that many of them have never directly connected with their customers, so even if the technology has enabled them to do just that, in many cases, they've hesitated to reach out.

Marketers understand the potential of social media marketing as a vital means of connecting with customers. In 2011, IBM surveyed more than 1,700 chief marketing officers (CMOs) to discover their top marketing priorities, both currently and over the next few years. There were two findings from this survey that

I want to highlight (http://www-935.ibm.com/services/us/cmo/ cmostudy2011/cmo-registration.html). First, 81 percent of the CMOs surveyed said that social media was the top technology that their company would focus on and shift marketing dollars to over the next three to five years. Second, the CMOs defined their top marketing priority in this digital era as *enhancing customer loyalty and brand advocacy.*

If you think about it, these two answers go together, don't they? There's no denying that the explosion of social media has gotten the attention of marketers worldwide, and with good reason. Suddenly, customers have the tools to quickly and easily create content, collaborate with friends and family to create content together, and share that content with others. The implications for marketers are staggering. What if those content creation tools were in the hands of an army of fans of your brand? What a powerful competitive advantage that could be, if only you knew how to utilize these new technologies in a way that drove real growth!

And this is the problem for many brands. Utilizing social media marketing and enhancing customer loyalty and advocacy continue to be priorities for brands mainly because most of them *can't figure out how to do either of these things effectively.* Marketers continue to focus on finding the ROI of social media simply because most of them can't tell whether their social media marketing efforts are actually working. Likewise, most marketers understand the significance of connecting with and embracing their brand's biggest fans, yet most of them have no idea how to do that. In doing research for this book, I talked to executives at several Fortune 500 companies because I wanted to learn more about their efforts to connect with their advocates and about the programs these brands had in place to stay connected to their most passionate customers.

What I learned surprised me. Not a single brand I talked to had a formal plan in place that connected it to its brand advocates. At best, a few brands monitored brand mentions and would connect with an individual customer if the brand felt that the situation warranted it. Thankfully, every brand said that although it didn't have a formal framework in place to connect with its fans, it would develop one if it knew how to implement such a process and program. *Think Like a Rock Star* will help them and you do just that. It will walk you through exactly how to use existing and emerging technologies like social media to connect with and cultivate fans of your brand, and then build on those lessons to show you how to become a truly fan-centric brand.

What to Expect from *Think Like a Rock Star*

This book is designed to teach you not only how to better connect with your fans by learning from what works for rock stars, but also how to become a rock star brand. I'll show you what rock stars do to cultivate and connect with their fans, and I'll teach you how to structure your organization so that you can better connect with your customers, turn them into fans, and capitalize on those interactions.

Throughout the book, I will place a heavy emphasis on case studies from both music and business. I will show you how rock stars do it, and then I'll give you an example of one or more brands that are using these very same tactics to connect with their most passionate customers. I've added links to relevant information that will help you learn more about the topic that's being discussed. Maybe this will be an article or a study, or perhaps it's a blog post. For your convenience, I've collected all these links in the Appendix and added the QR code to each.

For the remainder of this book, I will make you three promises:

1. I will show you what works.
2. I will explain to you why it works.
3. I will show you how to make it work for your brand.

While *Think Like a Rock Star* will show you how to use social media marketing to better cultivate fans of your brand, you won't see a lot of tool-specific advice. In other words, I'm not going to spend much time teaching you how to set up a Twitter account or a Facebook page, or how to get more retweets or Likes. The lessons you will learn on how to better connect with your existing fans and cultivate new ones will apply to all your marketing efforts, not just social media marketing. A piece of advice I always give clients is: *Don't focus on the tools. Focus on the connections that the tools help facilitate.* The tools are evolving constantly, and no doubt the list of "hot" social media tools will have changed between the time when I am writing this book and the time when you read it. I would rather teach you how to build connections and engagement with your customers via any form of social media marketing, so that you can leverage those connections into sales for your brand today—and also tomorrow. Perhaps my biggest goal as an author is to write a book that will continue to provide value to you as a marketer for many years to come.

Let me be clear: this book is going to challenge a lot of preconceived notions you may have about what successful marketing is and what it looks like. Many of the concepts we'll be discussing, especially those concerning how rock stars connect with their fans, may seem counterintuitive or downright confusing at first. I realize this, and it's a big reason why we'll look at case studies from both music and business, so that you can see how brands like your own are applying these same concepts in their marketing efforts.

Think Like a Rock Star is a passion project of mine. I've always been enamored with how rock stars have fans who truly love them. As a marketer, it's inspiring to see fans who care that deeply for their favorite artists. There's no reason why your brand cannot have the same relationship with your customers. I want that for your brand. This book will give you the road map for not only greatly improving your marketing efforts but creating an organization that helps you connect with your biggest advocates—and benefit from their love of your brand.

Let's get started!

Introduction

Let's say you are a marketing executive at a major record label, and your boss calls you into her office for a special project. She wants you to create a one-time concert for one of the label's up-and-coming artists. The artist has just released her debut album, and although she hasn't achieved mainstream success yet, she does have a small yet very passionate group of fans. Your boss wants this concert to galvanize the artist's fans, and to attract fans from all across the United States and even Canada. She adds that she wants the concert to be "an event that her fans will remember for the rest of their lives."

You return to your office, letting the enormous difficulty of creating such a "life-changing event" sink in for a couple of minutes. Then you start jotting down some ideas, and you realize that this won't be nearly as difficult as you thought. All you'll need to do is start a Facebook page for the event, and perhaps a blog; maybe you can reach out to the artist's fans via Twitter. Why, you can just use social media to get some neat viral marketing action happening, and this little baby will promote itself!

There's just one problem: this isn't taking place today. *It's happening in 1996.* Facebook doesn't exist. Neither do blogs, Twitter, or any other social media tools to get the word out about this special event.

Just when you are convinced that this project is impossible, your boss adds the final nail to your coffin: you have to find a way to convince the artist's fans to organize the concert themselves, including securing a suitable location for the event.

But you see, this story of a life-changing concert conceived and organized by one artist's fans isn't a fairy tale. It actually happened. And the story of how and why it happened can teach you an incredible amount about why rock stars have fans—and companies have customers.

In 1995, as Jewel's musical career was getting off the ground, one of her fans started an e-mail mailing list to connect with the artist's other fans. In the days before Facebook and MySpace, these lists were quite popular as a way for people around the country to stay connected to one another. Members would get regular e-mails that contained a digest of the e-mails from other members, and they could in turn respond to the messages left by others. Jewel was quite smart about this; she stayed closely connected to this small, but passionate group of her fans, and she was even known to occasionally post to the list herself. Jewel's manager/mom even dubbed these fans Jewel's "Everyday Angels" (or EDAs for short), after a line in one of Jewel's songs.

In the summer of 1996, the members of the list started talking about how great it would be if there were one amazing concert just for the EDAs (http://www.jeweljk.com/forum/index. php?topic=1093.0). As the members talked about this idea, they began to flesh out how it could happen, and they really got excited at the prospect of its possibly happening. A member of the list had a direct connection to Jewel's management, so the member reached out to her contact to see what Jewel thought of the idea.

In June of 1996, Jewel contacted the mailing list and told them that she would perform a free concert just for the list members. There was one huge catch, though: the list members had to organize the event and even secure the location for the concert, so that all Jewel had to do was show up and perform. This really wasn't a problem at all to the EDAs, who were absolutely thrilled at being given the responsibility for organizing all the details of the concert. The group quickly settled on a location in New York that was fairly close to the location of the original Woodstock concert in 1969. So naturally, the EDAs decided to dub this concert "JewelStock."

As word that the concert was actually happening spread quickly throughout the mailing list, members from all across the country and even Canada started saying that they wanted to attend. This posed another problem, as a lot of the EDAs from the West Coast and Canada would probably need some help in getting to JewelStock. The members decided to create a program called Angel Needs a Ride (also named after the title of one of Jewel's songs) that would help make sure that all the members who wanted to attend JewelStock could get a ride. The EDAs even created a separate website just for the Angel Needs a Ride program; it had local lodging information and contact information for all members who had agreed to give list members a ride if they needed one.

As the planning progressed, a list member secured artist Patti Griffin to be Jewel's opening act. All types of JewelStock merchandise were created, from buttons to T-shirts. Originally, Jewel had agreed to perform one concert, but so many non-EDAs had heard about the concert that she agreed to perform an additional concert the following night that would be open to the public. In total, she performed two concerts, totaling almost eight hours of music and 64 songs in two nights. Jewel also gave some of her biggest fans, from ages 15 to 50, some of the best concert memories of their lives. *She created something amazing for the people who loved her.*

Why do rock stars have fans and companies have customers? It comes down to how rock stars relate to their fans, as opposed to how companies connect with their customers. Most companies seek to have a transactional relationship with their customers. But many rock stars have an *emotional* relationship with their fans. They honestly care about their fans, want to be close to them, and appreciate their support. Even though Jewel wasn't getting paid to perform eight hours of music over two nights (not including staying for hours afterward each night to sign autographs and meet with the EDAs), she happily did so because she loved her fans. She had an *emotional* connection with her EDAs.

Let's look at how Jewel used this e-mail list to connect with her fans:

First, when Jewel realized that some of her fans had created this mailing list, she not only kept an eye on it, but occasionally participated in the list. Additionally, her manager (who was also her mom) and members of her management team posted to the list on occasion. This excited the list members and encouraged more participation and activity, as the knowledge that Jewel might be reading the messages they were leaving there was no doubt a big thrill for the list members!

Second, she gave her fans an identity. She called them her Everyday Angels, a nod to a line from her song "I'm Sensitive." This alone gave these fans a sense of having a closer connection with Jewel, and also gave them a reason to care for her more deeply.

Third, when Jewel was approached with the idea of performing a concert just for her EDAs, not only did she agree, but she gave her fans ownership of the project. This was a brilliant move on Jewel's part. She could no doubt tell how deeply her fans wanted this concert to take place, and so she empowered them to create it. Then, after weeks of planning and organizing by hundreds of fans, having Jewel perform almost eight hours of music for them over two nights had to be an incredible event for the fans to be a part of. In a way, Jewel's fans planning and organizing the concert, then Jewel performing at it, could be seen as both Jewel and her fans expressing their love for each other.

As a brand marketer, does this scenario sound impossible to you? While brands have been struggling for decades to create marketing that resonates and to build relationships with their customers, building relationships comes quite naturally to rock stars. Rock stars frequently cultivate fans who not only are frequent customers but also quite literally fall in love with their favorite rock stars.

"But Mack, you're talking about rock stars! Rock stars will always have fans more easily than brands, simply because, well... they're rock stars!"

Think about it. When you download a song off the Internet, do you consider yourself to be a fan or a customer of that rock star? You probably view yourself as a fan, right? Now, the next time you go grocery shopping, think about the items you buy. Do you consider yourself a fan or a customer of most of those brands? If you're like me, you tend to view yourself as a fan of rock stars and a customer of most brands.

Why is this? When I first started tackling this question a few years ago, I thought I knew the answer. I assumed it must simply be because rock stars create entertaining products. Music, videos, T-shirts—these are all products that we love, right? As I started researching how rock stars market themselves and how they connect with their customers, however, I began to realize that it wasn't just through the products that they create. Repeatedly, I came across stories like JewelStock. These stories clearly demonstrated how rock stars appreciate and even *love* their fans. Rock stars do very real things that make it easier for them to cultivate fans.

The more I examined the contrast between how rock stars and brands market themselves and connect with their customers, the more I understood why rock stars have fans and companies have customers. The answer is surprisingly simple: *because that's what both groups want.* Rock stars want to connect with their existing fans and cultivate new ones, while most companies place a priority on acquiring new customers. Rock stars have fans because they want fans, and companies have customers because they want customers. I even drew a neat sketch of what this relationship looks like. I call it the Loyalty Graph:

The Loyalty Graph

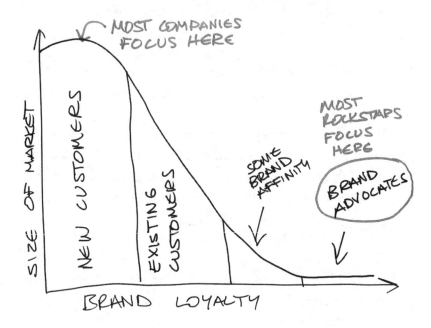

On the Loyalty Graph, the *x* axis represents brand loyalty, and the *y* axis represents size of market. Most companies are focused on acquiring new customers, and when you see the size of the market for new customers, you can understand why. New customers is by far the largest customer segment, so of course companies would want to acquire customers from this segment.

Yet while targeting new customers makes excellent sense when you consider size of market, you also have to consider the level of brand loyalty for this group. New customers might be the biggest market segment, but if you are a company that is trying to acquire new customers, you also have to consider that this group has the *lowest levels of brand loyalty.* New customers have little to no affinity for your brand; in fact, you might even call them indifferent to your brand. So even if you can acquire a new customer, since she has little or no loyalty to your brand, there's no guarantee that you can hold on to her past that initial purchase. This also helps to explain why the cost to acquire new customers is so high for brands. There's a high churn rate, due in great part to the fact that this group has little to no brand loyalty.

Now let's re-examine the Loyalty Graph and look at how rock stars position their marketing efforts. Note that rock stars, for the most part, aren't focused on acquiring new customers; their area of focus is on the opposite end of the x axis. Rock stars focus on connecting with their *existing fans*. Looking at the Loyalty Graph, you can see two key differences between brand advocates/fans and new customers:

1. Fans are a much smaller group. In fact, they are by far the smallest group of customers.
2. Fans have *extreme* levels of brand loyalty.

As a brand marketer, you might look at this graph and think that while it's great to connect with fans, since the group is so small, it's not worth the effort. You might think it's better to go after acquiring new customers, even if you realize that the high churn rate will force up the cost of marketing to this group.

But here's the important point to consider: since fans have extreme levels of brand loyalty, not only will they keep buying your brand, but they will also actively encourage *other* customers to buy it as well. So your brand's fans are the special customers that love your brand so much that they will tell those customers who have some brand affinity, your existing customers, and your new customers that they need to stick with your brand. And the best part? Your fans are *acquiring new customers for you.* Think about it: Which is more likely to compel you to try a brand's products, a commercial that you see during this week's episode of your favorite detective drama, or a referral from a friend who is a big fan of that brand? Your friend's passionate endorsement will win you over almost every time, unlike a commercial that very possibly airs while you are in the bathroom.

Rock stars have always understood this. They place such an emphasis on connecting with their existing fans because they realize that their ability to bring in new customers tomorrow is based in great part on their ability to delight their existing fans *today.* In the end, both companies and rock stars acquire new customers. It's just that rock stars do so mainly by connecting with their biggest fans, whereas companies do so mainly by spending too much money on ineffective marketing. A new customer who is acquired through a referral from a trusted friend is more likely to become a regular customer than a new customer who is acquired through marketing alone.

A rock star who illustrates the power of connecting with her fans, especially via social media, is Amanda Palmer. Let me share with you one example of how Amanda energizes and excites her fans.

One Friday night in 2011, I was on Twitter, and I saw several of the people I follow tweeting excitedly about an Amanda Palmer show that they had attended that night in Boston. Many of these people were saying that it was one of the best shows they had ever seen, and a few of them even called it a life-changing experience.

Interested in learning more, I clicked over to read Amanda's updates, and I saw her tweeting about a secret show that she had put on that night in Boston. I did some checking, and it seems that Amanda had used the social networking/entertainment site Get Glue to organize this secret show. What she did was ask her fans who wanted to attend the show to go to her profile page on Get Glue and leave a comment about their favorite moment at an Amanda Palmer concert or show. This was the only requirement to be eligible to receive a free ticket to the show.

What's interesting about this approach is that Amanda not only gave away tickets to the show, but structured the giveaway so that her biggest and most loyal fans would have an advantage. Those of Amanda's fans who had attended the most shows and who had seen Amanda perform over the course of her career would have more interesting experiences from these performances to share. This approach no doubt seems completely counterintuitive to many marketers, especially the ones that focus on acquiring *new* customers. Not only did Amanda focus on her existing customers with this secret show, but she also gave away the tickets to her biggest fans—the very customers who were the most likely to want to *buy* tickets to an Amanda Palmer concert.

Yet she also did something else: she created *something amazing for the people who love her*. By targeting her biggest fans with this secret show, Amanda found a way to thrill and delight the people who cared most about her. Whereas many marketers would look at this as a huge missed opportunity to sell tickets to these fans, Amanda saw the word-of-mouth marketing potential of delighting her biggest fans with a free show. This gave those fans yet another reason to go out and promote Amanda to others. Amanda may not have generated sales at this event, but the positive word of mouth created by fans who attended the event will no doubt lead to future sales for the artist.

Now I can hear a cynical marketer responding with, "So you're saying that this rock star tweeted to her fans that she was giving away tickets to a show, and was able to give them all away? Wow, that's impressive; what else ya got?"

In May 2012, Amanda launched a project on Kickstarter to fund a tour to promote her new album and art book (http://www.kickstarter.com/projects/amandapalmer/amanda-palmer-the-new-record-art-book-and-tour). Kickstarter is a site that gives entrepreneurs the chance to raise money for their projects and/or products, without having to create the product first. For example, if you think you can create the best digital music player on the market, you can create a project on Kickstarter to fund the creation of the player. Let's say you need to raise $50,000 to create the player. You set that as your funding goal, and you offer your backers the chance to buy the product after you have created it. If your project reaches its funding goal (meaning that enough backers commit to buy your product), then you take that funding and create the product. If you don't reach your funding goal, then you don't have to make the product.

Amanda created her project with a funding goal of $100,000, which is pretty high for a Kickstarter project. She accepted backers at several different financial levels, offering everything from a digital download of one song for $1 at the low end, all the way up to the $10,000 level, which included dinner with Amanda along with her drawing your portrait and some other cool prizes. As you might expect, Amanda reached out to her fans via social media sites like Twitter and her blog to help her promote her Kickstarter project and let them become backers if they were interested. Amanda's project had 31 days to reach her funding goal of $100,000.

The results? When the project closed on May 31, 2012, almost 25,000 backers had pledged a grand total of $1,192,793 to fund Amanda's project. This exceeded Amanda's required funding level by *more than $1 million* and made it one of the most successful projects ever on Kickstarter. That's not a bad return on an investment of connecting with and embracing your fans via social media, is it?

Amanda Palmer is able to leverage social media and emerging technologies to connect with her fans because she has *always strived to connect with her fans.* Even before the technology that would facilitate those connections was available, rock stars like Amanda have always found ways to become more closely connected to their fans.

Which begs the question, why haven't most brands made that same commitment to building strong relationships with their fans? In short, brands have never had to connect directly with their fans because their fans have never had an effective way to connect directly with the brand. But social media have changed the communication dynamic between the brand and the consumers. Now, customers have the ability to create content about brands quickly and easily, and they can connect with one another and share their thoughts and opinions about any brand that they choose.

What this means for your brand is that the game has changed. When it comes to communication, in just a few short years, the balance of power has shifted toward the consumer. If your brand can begin to develop closer connections with its most passionate

BACKSTAGE PASS!

IF YOU ATTEND concerts, you know that a backstage pass is gold. It allows you to go backstage to meet the rock star and his band and watch them rehearse. Basically, it's a way to pull back the curtain and see the magic that's happening behind the scenes.

Throughout *Think Like a Rock Star*, you'll find a backstage pass like this in each chapter. These will give you tips to immediately utilize the concepts and ideas that we are discussing to better connect with and cultivate fans of your brand. We'll pull back the curtain and let you see how this stuff works so that you can start improving your social media and marketing strategies right now.

Here's your first pass: start identifying your current fans. Note how Amanda Palmer is cultivating new fans by connecting with her existing ones. You can do the exact same thing, but you need to figure out who your *current* fans are before you can start connecting with them.

How do you do this? Look for hand raisers. Look for customers who have taken the initiative and contacted your brand. Talk to the people on your customer service team and see if they've come in contact, via e-mail or phone or carrier pigeon, with any customers that they feel may be fans of your brand. Ask them to please let you know if they connect with any customers in the future that they feel could be fans of your brand. Look online and see what customers are saying about your brand on forums and social media sites. See if you can identify a few customers who appear to be fans.

continued...

> While you are compiling your list, here's an important point to remember: the size of the list does *not* matter. Sure, it would be great if you could create a list of 1,000 customers who are fans of your brand, but the process of actually *connecting* with your fans is far more important than how many fans you have. The key point is that you are taking the first steps toward having a connection and ultimately a relationship with your fans. So if your first list of fans has only five names on it, that doesn't matter. Simply starting down the path of connecting with and cultivating fans of your brand is what's most important, and you've just taken that first step! So make your list of fans, then look for additional backstage passes as you continue reading. We'll begin to build on the good work that you've started.

customers, not only will you see immediate business benefits, but you will also enjoy a significant advantage over your competitors who are still clinging to an outdated model of customer relationship management.

Think Like a Rock Star is going to walk you through the process rock stars have used for decades to cultivate fans and then show you how to apply these same ideas to your own fan-building efforts. Over the course of the first four chapters, we will talk about four reasons rock stars have fans instead of customers:

1. Rock stars are fans themselves.
2. Rock stars look for ways to shift control to their fans.
3. Rock stars find the "Bigger Idea" behind the music they create.
4. Rock stars embrace and empower their fans.

PART I

THE FOUR REASONS ROCK STARS HAVE FANS (AND YOUR COMPANY HAS CUSTOMERS)

CHAPTER 1

Rock Stars Are Fans Themselves

Perhaps the biggest reason why rock stars have fans instead of customers is that rock stars are fans themselves. Think about it. Rock stars are obviously going to be fans of their own music, right? This means that they are, by definition, members of the very audience they are trying to connect with. This also allows them to have a deeper level of understanding of their fans. Add the fact that rock stars are constantly connecting directly with their fans via concerts and appearances, and you can see how easily rock stars not only understand their fans but feel an actual emotional connection with these special people. The following example perfectly illustrates how rock stars understand their fans and their point of view.

Nettwerk Defends a Music Fan Accused of Stealing Its Artists' Music

In 2006, David Greubel received a rather ominous letter from the Recording Industry Association of America (RIAA), the music industry's governing body. The RIAA was contacting Mr. Greubel to let him know that it was seeking a judgment against him because it believed that Mr. Greubel's home computer had been used to illegally download songs off the Internet. Some of the songs that the RIAA believed had been illegally downloaded were performed by artists that were being managed by Terry McBride, who was the CEO of Nettwerk Music, a music label based in Canada.

When Terry found out that the RIAA was pursuing legal action against Mr. Greubel, he immediately got involved in the process—but not in the way you might think. Nettwerk Music contacted Mr. Greubel and informed him that if he would fight this case in court, Nettwerk would agree to pay any and all legal fees and judgments associated with the case. The case did indeed go to court and was eventually settled, with Nettwerk paying all associated fees.

Why in the world would Nettwerk essentially turn its back on its own industry to support a music fan who was accused of stealing music from its own artists? Because Nettwerk felt that the RIAA was ultimately hurting its artists by suing music fans. Nettwerk was able to look at this situation through the eyes of the artists' fans. Terry understood that while supporting legal action such as this might result in a few dollars for his artists in the short term, it would probably erode the trust between his artists and their fans in the long run. He was willing to side with the music fans, even if it meant drawing the ire of many of his peers.

As you're thinking about how you can become better connected with your customers and cultivate fans of your brand, please keep the following in mind at all times. Your customers won't become fans of your brand unless *they understand your brand and feel that your brand understands them.* Only when this happens will they begin to let their guard down and trust you. Once that trust between your customers and your brand has been established, they may begin to *advocate* for your brand.

Terry McBride understood that when they shared music online, music fans weren't trying to hurt the artists that his label managed; they just wanted more access to more music. He also understood that you shouldn't attempt to legislate the behavior of teenagers! His position was that he needed to understand and accept the behavior of his fans, and to think about ways to work with it instead of against it. This is why he's opposed to the RIAA suing music fans, and why he supports services like Spotify that make it easier and cheaper for fans to get access to more music. As a result, music fans develop greater respect for Nettwerk and are more loyal to its artists. So if your brand wants to cultivate fans, then you need not only to gain a deeper level of understanding of who your customers are, but to help them understand your brand and what it stands for as well.

A few years ago I saw a cable special on the Harley-Davidson brand. Harley-Davidson is what many people would consider a rock star brand. The host was talking to a Harley-Davidson executive about the company's marketing efforts and whether the brand did a lot of market research in an effort to better understand its customers. The executive immediately noted that Harley-Davidson was in constant contact with its customers because its employees *rode with them all the time.* The point this executive was making was that Harley-Davidson doesn't need to consult a spreadsheet or hire a team of business consultants to learn who its customers are. The company understands its customers because *they are part of the same community.* Its executives love their motorcycles just as much as their customers do, and they enjoy using them in the same ways their customers do and interacting with their customers. Simply interacting with customers on the open road, even if it's only a few at a time, gives Harley-Davidson's executives key insights into who the company's customers are and why they buy its products.

So if you want to better understand your customers, you need to become better connected to them, and they to you. Luckily, the rise of social media and digital technologies has made it easier than ever before for you to interact with your customers and better understand them. For example, I just did a Google search for Harley-Davidson, and there are more than 160 million results! No doubt buried in these results are thousands of Facebook pages, groups, forums, and message boards run by fans of Harley-Davidson. Now granted, your brand may not be as big as Harley-Davidson, but the odds are that your current and potential customers are online and creating content about your brand and your marketplace. That content might be on their blogs, on LinkedIn Groups, or on Twitter. The point is, the content is out there, and it gives you a wonderful chance to learn more about who your customers are and how and why they buy your products. We'll do a deep dive into how you can monitor the online conversations your customers are having in Chapters 7 and 8.

For right now, start by simply Googling your brand and your competitors. Then start doing the same searches with Google Blog Search, which will show you what bloggers are saying about your brand and your marketplace (http://www.google.com/blogsearch). Another site you may find useful is Boardreader.com, which is a search engine for posting on message boards and forums (http://boardreader.com/). Start playing around with these free online search engines and you'll start to get an idea of the conversations that are happening online that involve your brand and your marketplace. This is a very simple method that you can start using *today* to get a better understanding of what your online customers are saying about your brand.

Graco Creates a Successful Blogging Strategy Powered by the Same Audience It Wants to Reach

If your brand wants to cultivate fans, it pays to be part of the same community that you are trying to connect with. Rock stars have always done a wonderful job of this, and it's possible for your brand to do the same.

A perfect example of this is how Graco structured its strategy for its blog when it launched it in 2008. When Graco was ready to launch a company blog, the brand decided to first invest several months in monitoring online mentions of its brand. It took this approach because not only did it want to understand the online conversations that were happening that involved its brand, but it also wanted to discover who was participating in those conversations.

Finally, Graco was ready to launch its blogging strategy. In my mind, there are three key elements that made this strategy so successful. First, Graco needed to decide who the target audience for its blog was. After spending several months monitoring the online conversations involving its brand, Graco determined that the primary audience for its blog would be young parents with young children. That was the first step.

Then it decided that the content on its new blog would focus on parenting and would deal with issues and situations that its target audience was grappling with every single day. Too many companies create content on their blogs that's very self-promotional. The end result is that the company's blog becomes little more than a digital version of its weekly circular. Graco could promote its products on its blog, but it would do so in the context of discussing the larger topic of parenting, which is far more valuable to its readers.

Now Graco knew whom it was writing for (young parents with young children) and the focus of the blog's content (parenting). The final element of its blogging strategy that Graco needed to decide on was who would write the blog. This is where Graco had a stroke of genius. The company decided that since it wanted to write parenting content for young parents with young children, why not pick bloggers who were… young parents with young children? Graco was smart enough to pick bloggers who belonged to the community that the brand wanted to connect with. Readers of Graco's blog are more likely to pay attention to the content because it's written from a point of view that's familiar to them: their own. The content resonates because it addresses situations and problems that the readers are already dealing with.

How successful has this blogging strategy been for Graco? As of 2007, 68 percent of all online mentions of the Graco brand were positive. A year after Graco launched its blog, that figure had ballooned to 83 percent, and total online mentions of the brand had *doubled* at the same time. By becoming an active participant in the online conversations about its brand, Graco had changed those conversations.

Note that the brand started by doing research to determine *who* was talking about the brand online and *what those people were saying.* With those findings, the brand could flesh out its content strategy and determine who would blog for the brand. But the foundation of its successful blogging strategy came from Graco's first investing the time to learn as much as possible about the conversations that were happening online involving its brand. By doing this, the company began to *understand* the people who were involved in those conversations. The impact that understanding your customers and their point of view has on your marketing and its effectiveness cannot be overstated.

Earlier we talked about how Harley-Davidson executives connect with their customers by riding the open road with them. In much the same way, Tim League makes a point of watching movies in his theaters alongside his customers. This allows him to enjoy the same experience they have and better understand what shapes that experience, as this example shows.

Alamo Drafthouse Throws Customers Out; Movie Fans Love It

Let's make a quick list of some of the things that annoy us when we're watching a movie at a theater:

1. People who talk loudly during the movie
2. People who talk on their phones during the movie
3. People who text on their phones during the movie

Alamo Drafthouse CEO Tim League agrees and even trains the ushers at his movie theaters to throw out any customer who is engaging in behavior that's distracting or bothersome to the other moviegoers. In 1997, League adopted a strict no talking policy at Alamo Drafthouse. He realized that some patrons would be upset about the policy, and might even take their business elsewhere. So why did League adopt such policies at his theaters? He did this because he is a fan of watching movies at theaters, and of the experience that's unique to that setting. As a fan, he knows what behavior distracts from that experience, and he has policies in place to ensure that such behavior isn't tolerated.

In 2009, Tim attended one of his theaters and helped throw out a customer who was talking during the movie. The customer then followed Tim to his car and hit his windshield! League blogged about the event, and not only refused to apologize for his actions, but clearly stated that the customer was welcome to *never* come back to his theater!

What's been the reaction to Alamo Drafthouse's no talking or texting policies? It's been overwhelmingly positive. In 2011, a teenager was booted from an Alamo Drafthouse theater for texting on her phone. Shortly afterward, she left a profanity-laced voicemail at the theater complaining about being kicked out of the theater. Alamo Drafthouse took her voicemail and turned it into a video that is shown before movies. Here's the video, and, warning, it does use profanity: http://www.youtube.com/watch?v=1L3eeC2lJZs.

After it was posted on YouTube, the video went viral and drew millions of views. It garnered national media attention for Alamo Drafthouse and its CEO, whom Anderson Cooper called a "great American hero" for kicking out the texter (http://blogs.indiewire.com/thompsononhollywood/alamo_drafthouses_kicked_out_customer_worst_moviegoer_ever#).

Alamo Drafthouse's customers love League's strict policies about behavior during a movie because they understand that he's trying to create a better viewing experience for everyone. League is

BACKSTAGE PASS!

IN THE BACKSTAGE PASS in the Introduction, we talked about how you should begin the process of attempting to identify your brand's fans. Hopefully, you've now started putting together that list. The next step is to leverage your list of fans to get a better sense of who they are and what type of connection and relationship they could have with your brand.

For example, let's say you have identified 10 bloggers that you believe are fans of your brand. All of these bloggers have written about your brand, probably in a positive light, and possibly they have even stated that they are fans of your brand. At this point, you want to do two things:

1. You want to acknowledge them and *thank* them for their advocacy of your brand.
2. You want to find a way to start an ongoing dialogue with them.

The first step is imperative. It could be something as simple as sending each blogger an e-mail thanking him for his support. This might seem a bit trivial, but to a true advocate, getting attention from his or her favorite brand is a big deal! By thanking your bloggers for their support, you are also giving them an incentive to continue to promote your brand to others.

Second, you want to find a way to have a continuing dialogue with your fans. Increasingly, brands are paying more attention to the power of connecting with their advocates. However, too many brands are excited about reaching out to their brand advocates because they love the idea of having a way to "let our advocates tell our story." It's true that advocates want to promote you, but to view the potential of advocates as being strictly promotional is incredibly shortsighted. Your brand wants to build an ongoing relationship with your fans in order to maximize the potential of those connections.

For example, in 2010, I played a small role in helping Dell launch its CAP program. CAP stands for Customer Advisory Panel, and what Dell did was identify 15 or so advocates for Dell that it found online. Dell occasionally invites these fans to Austin so that its executives can talk to them directly, but Dell communicates with them online as well. One way Dell has done this is by creating a private LinkedIn Group just for its CAP members. This allows Dell to connect directly with its fans and ask for their unfiltered feedback. It can ask the group how it could improve its products and services, what the group thinks of particular products that it sells, and similar questions. By making the effort to find and connect with its fans, Dell now has a program in place that allows it to connect directly with its fans and to learn from them, as well as to empower them to advocate on Dell's behalf.

This is a very simple example and something that your brand can easily replicate. It doesn't have to be a LinkedIn Group; it could just as easily be a Facebook group or a website that you set up. Even a good old-fashioned e-mail list would work in this case. The key point is to start building a way to connect directly with your brand's fans.

approaching this as a movie fan, not as a CEO. This is a big reason why Alamo Drafthouse is so popular with movie fans who want to watch movies in a theater. They know that if they go to Alamo Drafthouse, they will get a better experience because League is working hard to ensure it.

If you can find ways to improve your customers' experience and environment, you are communicating to them that you understand their point of view. This is an incredibly powerful way to connect with your customers, earn their loyalty, and cultivate fans.

How Does Your Brand Become Part of the Same Community as Your Fans?

Rock stars have an inherent advantage over most brands when it comes to connecting with their fans in that they *want* to connect with their fans. They thrive on connecting with their fans. As a result, they better understand their fans, and their fans better understand them.

If your brand is at a place where you are disconnected from your customers, what do you do? Recall that in the Graco example, the brand invested months in monitoring and tracking the online conversations that its customers were having. Its goal was to *understand* who its customers were and what was important to them. Sure, Graco had probably done customer surveys and had a good idea of who its customers were and what was important to them, but it wanted to know what its customers were talking about right now, and *what role the brand could play in those conversations*.

This is a key distinction. Graco wasn't trying to control the conversations its customers were having, nor was it trying to ignore those conversations. It wanted to be an *active participant* in those conversations. Its blog gave the brand a vehicle that allowed it to become a part of the community it was trying to connect with. By doing so, Graco now had a voice in the ongoing conversations that involved its brand.

It pays to invest the time in understanding who your customers are and what motivates them. Please keep in mind that this goes beyond simply monitoring online conversations. You need to pay close attention to offline communications that your customers send you. What are your customers saying in the letters they send you or during their phone calls? Even if these communications are complaints about your brand, pay close attention to why your customers are complaining. What are they saying about the things in their daily lives that prompted them to reach out to you? For example, if a customer writes to tell you that your toaster intermittently fails and adds, "As a single mother of three, I am rushing to get my children off to school every morning, and I don't have time for this!" you've just been given valuable clues to this customer's life and lifestyle. It pays to dig deeper and get real insights into who your customers are, because that will give you ideas about how you can create value for them.

Always Think About How You Can Create Value for Your Customers

In the Graco example, the company did extensive research to determine who its target audience was and understand how it could create value for them. Think of this as Graco's admission ticket into this community. By creating content that was valuable to this group, Graco earned its attention.

I just gave an example of a single mom of three writing your brand a letter to complain about a toaster that you sell. Let's say your brand sells different types of kitchen appliances. You start researching the feedback you are getting from your customers on your appliances. You consider letters written to your company, blog posts, Amazon reviews, and even tweets on Twitter. After spending a few months compiling the responses from your customers, you note that in 23 percent of the responses, there is some mention of how your products either save time for your customers or waste time for them when the products fail. Additionally, 38 percent of the customer feedback on your products contains some mention of using the product in the preparation of a particular meal. In those cases, 78 percent of these responses mention using these products to make breakfast.

When you examine the research, it may indicate that your products are popular with parents who are trying to save time, especially when they are making breakfast for their children. There's your value proposition for the content that you will create. You want to create content that shows parents how to create healthy meals for their families quickly. And since these parents are already strapped for time, showing them how to create meals that can be cleaned up quickly would probably be a nice touch as well! You could even expand this to add an offline element by creating in-person events where chefs cook healthy meals for families in 30 minutes or less, using your products.

By adopting this strategy, you are creating content that's crafted from your customer's point of view. The customer's core problem isn't, "How do I buy more of your cooking products?" It's, "How do I cook a healthy meal for my family in less than 30 minutes that can also be cleaned up quickly?" If you are solving the customer's core problem, you are giving her a reason to purchase your products. This makes your content more customer-centric, which makes it more relevant to the people you are trying to reach. This, in turn, increases the loyalty of these customers, which makes them more likely to tell others about your products.

Here is an age-old marketing truism: sell the benefit, not the product. When you sell the benefit, your marketing will have more relevance for your customers because it will speak to them in a voice that's more like their own. This also increases the chance that your customers will not only pay attention to what you are saying, but share what you are saying with others (driving increased customer loyalty).

So far, we've talked about becoming more closely connected to your brand's fans by better understanding them, and by creating content and marketing that speaks to their wants and needs, rather than simply promoting yourself. But in order to truly become a part of their community, you need to stay connected to them. In the Graco example, by creating a blog, the brand gave its customers a way to contact it directly via comments on the blog. Graco can have a better understanding of how its content is resonating with its target market by checking the comments it gets from its readers. The idea here is to create a way for the brand to directly connect with its fans, and vice versa.

continues contact

The Five Keys to Becoming More Connected to Your Customers and Fans

Let's recap what we've discussed so far in this chapter and boil it down to five key steps.

1. You need to better understand who your customers and fans are.

You want to understand who your customers are, what motivates them, and what they are looking for. Recall that in the Graco example, it wasn't until the brand had done its research that it determined exactly who its blog's target audience was (young parents with young children) and what the members of that audience were looking for (help with parenting issues).

For example, let's say your brand sells lawn-care products and wants to start a blog to use as a tool to build awareness of your products. One way to connect with the customers that you want to be reading your blog is to find out where they are spending their time online and follow them there. In other words, where are they going to find the answers to their lawn-care questions and problems? If you can identify, say, three or four sites or blogs that are popular resources for customers with lawn-care questions and problems, it makes sense for you to participate on those sites by leaving comments and helping other customers by answering their questions. That way, not only can you learn more about the wants and needs of your customers, but by interacting with them, you are giving your customers a reason to check out your blog! If Tim posts a comment to a post on a lawn-care site and you give him a useful answer, not only have you given Tim a reason to pay attention to you and your blog, but you've also provided value for other people who read your answer to Tim's question. The key is to figure out where the people that you want to have reading your blog are currently getting their information; you can then go to those same sites and interact with them there. This will not only help you better understand them, but give you a chance to better connect with them as well.

2. Change your marketing and promotional efforts to create more value for your customers and fans.

Instead of trying to use the same marketing channels to connect with your customers and fans, build on the insights gained into who these people are, and tailor your communication efforts so that they resonate with your customers.

Sometimes the best marketing doesn't look like marketing at all. When Warner Bros. was promoting the movie *The Dark Knight*, it put together all the standard online and offline marketing promotions that you would expect to see for a summer blockbuster. But the marketing campaign for *The Dark Knight* also had an element of fun to it. Warner Bros. created an elaborate online marketing campaign, one element of which required you to decode online websites that tied into the movie. If you were the first person from your area to decipher the website, you would be given the address of a local bakery that was holding a cake for you to pick up under the name Robbin Banks (robbin' banks, get it?). When you received the cake, the icing said, "Call Me Now," and included a phone number. If you dialed the number, the cake itself started ringing! Inside the cake was a packet containing a cell phone and other items from the company Rent a Clown, apparently set up by Batman's archenemy in the movie, the Joker!

Campaigns such as this were great fun for fans of *The Dark Knight,* and helped create a lot of extra buzz around the film (http://www.youtube.com/watch?v=7ibFOA6c5Zk).

3. Look at the world through the eyes of your fans and customers.

Once you've followed Steps 1 and 2 and have a better understanding of who your fans and customers are and what their wants and needs are, you need to create marketing communications that address *their* wants and needs, not your own. Harley-Davidson executives are constantly riding their Harleys with other owners, so they can talk to them directly and look at the open road through their eyes. They understand that the Harley brand is as much (or even more!) about a lifestyle as it is about a motorcycle. Harley-Davidson's marketing efforts reflect this. Tim League, CEO of Alamo Drafthouse, kicks customers out of his theaters if they are being noisy and disruptive during movies. Tim is willing to lose the business of these customers because he understands what his fans want, and he knows that by kicking out disruptive customers, he will be creating a better viewing experience *for his fans.*

4. Fish where the fish are.

When you are trying to better connect with your customers, especially your online customers, it pays to interact with them in their space. Think about what the sources of information in your industry or your space are, and start spending time on these sites, interacting with other users there. For example, if I want to make a name for myself as a social media consultant, I should start becoming active on sites like Mashable and Social Media Examiner, because these sites are where many people go to get the latest social media news and to learn more about social media marketing. If I spend time leaving valuable comments on Mashable, I will increase the likelihood that Mashable's readers will follow me back to my blog and start reading it! A key ingredient in building engagement around your social media marketing efforts is to connect with your audience members in *their* space on terms that are convenient to *them*, not to you.

5. Show your customers that you're human.

Believe it or not, your fans want to go behind the scenes and see what's going on "backstage" at your company, just as fans do at a concert. "People want to see what's behind the curtain more than ever these days," explains Katie Morse, who manages social media for *Billboard*. "Musicians have taken to Instagram en masse, just as an example, and many share photos of life on tour or even their daily lives (Rihanna, Drake, etc.). This content is *gold* in fans' eyes. Who doesn't want to see what Drake's hotel room in Cannes looks like, or what Rihanna really gets up to on a 'night out with the girls'? The same thing should apply to your brand. No, not everyone cares to see photos of worker bees in cubicles, but we *do* want to take a peek into how your bottled beverage is really put together, or what the raw ingredients for my favorite meal at a restaurant really look like."

Also keep in mind that by pulling back the curtain and allowing your customers to go "backstage," you are letting your guard down, a sign that you trust your customers. This makes it easier, in turn, for your customers to trust you, which makes it easier for them to become fans that advocate on behalf of your brand.

CHAPTER 2

Rock Stars Look for Ways
to Shift Control to Their Fans

One of the biggest reasons rock stars have fans rather than customers is that they look for ways to shift control to their fans and involve them in their marketing and communication processes. We talked about this a bit in the previous chapter, but most rock stars literally thrive on interacting with their fans, and that extends to their marketing and communication efforts.

This is in sharp contrast to the way many companies try to keep their customers at arm's length. The closest many brands come to involving their customers in the marketing and product creation process is crowdsourcing their Super Bowl commercials. Smart brands understand the power of word-of-mouth marketing and not only welcome their fans singing their praises to other customers, but actively look for ways to facilitate this happening.

This is something that rock stars have always understood. They view their fans as marketing partners. They see their fans are special people who are helping them promote and extend their brand, so they openly embrace their fans' existing efforts and look for ways to have a deeper connection with them.

The Donnas' Fans Create a Site to Share Their Music; the Band Loves It

Several years ago I was researching an article I was writing on music marketing, and I stumbled across a site called thedonnasmedia.com (http://thedonnasmedia.com/). If you are a fan of the band The Donnas, this site is your nirvana. It has literally thousands of audio and video files of the band's performances spanning its entire career. We are talking about everything from 30-second commercials that aired on radio stations in Pittsburgh to full-length concerts from Germany. You can even download full-length concerts and burn them onto CDs, and the fan-run site will provide you with the liner notes and graphics for your CDs!

My first thought was that this site was really awesome, and that fans of The Donnas would absolutely love it. My second thought was that as soon as The Donnas finds out about this site, its lawyers will send a cease-and-desist letter to the site, and it will disappear. So I did some checking, and it turns out that The Donnas is well aware of thedonnasmedia.com. In fact, the band not only knows about the site, but actively *encourages* its fans to check it out. Additionally, if the site is missing a certain performance by The Donnas, the band will encourage any fan who has a good copy of the performance to upload it to the site.

Why in the world would The Donnas do this? When I first discovered this site, back in 2006, I asked the band's manager at the time to explain the band's thinking in allowing so much of its music to be so readily available on the site. She told me that The Donnas saw the site as a way to grow its fan base, and it trusted its fans not to abuse the availability of the music. She added that the trust The Donnas has in its fans is a big reason why it has such a great relationship with them!

Also, there's a huge caveat to note with regard to the content on thedonnasmedia.com. The site is run by fans of the band, and they will allow no content on the site that's been commercially released by the band. So if you go there thinking that you can download the band's latest album, forget it. But if you live in Birmingham and want to download the audio from the concert you attended last week, there's a good chance that the site either has the performance or will shortly.

What I love about this story is how The Donnas views this site. The band doesn't view thedonnasmedia.com as something that's stealing sales from it, but instead sees it as a channel through which the band can get more fans because it's being developed and maintained by the band's *current* fans. The Donnas trusts its fans and has a great relationship with them, so it views them as partners who are helping it gain exposure to potential fans. Both The Donnas and its fans who run the site have the same goal: creating a way to introduce new fans to more music from the band they love.

If your fans feel a sense of ownership in your brand, they will act in what they perceive to be your brand's best interests. Rock stars understand this, which is a big reason why they are in constant contact and communication with their fans. They are constantly giving their fans a here's-how-you-can-help-us reminder. The more connection and communication a rock star has with his fans, the greater the chance that his fans will help promote the rock star in a way that benefits him. In this example, The Donnas is in contact with the owners of thedonnasmedia.com, and the band and the site owners share the same goal: to grow the fan base.

This is exactly why it benefits your brand to be in direct contact with your fans. Your fans want input from you on how they can help you promote your brand and grow your customer base. Your fans *want* this direction from you, because they want to act in a way that will ultimately help your brand.

If you embrace your fans and communicate with them, you'll discover that even when you create something that will benefit them, they will use it as a tool to help you.

Katy Perry Creates a Way for Her Fans to Share Who Their Firework Is

In 2010, singer Katy Perry decided to create a video contest to promote her new single, "Firework." Now before I talk about how Katy structured this contest, let's put on our marketing hats for a minute and think about how we might want to see this contest unfold.

If we were creating a video contest to promote our latest single in which our fans were creating the videos, how would we want it to be structured? Would we ask our fans to create their own version of the "Firework" video? Or what if we had our fans make videos of themselves singing "Firework" and we picked the best ones? With either method, our fans would be creating content that promotes us.

But that's not the approach Katy Perry took. If you've ever heard the song "Firework," you know that it speaks to certain themes. One is that everyone is beautiful in her own way—and to someone else. Another is that we all have a light to shine and that we can each make the world a brighter place in our own unique way. Katy wanted to structure the contest so that the videos would reflect these themes. So instead of asking her fans to create videos that promoted Katy and the song "Firework," she took a different approach.

Katy asked her fans to create videos telling the world who their Firework was. In other words, you had to tell the world who was special to you, someone who inspired you to become a better person and to see the world as a more positive place—someone who made the world a better place for you and everyone he or she came in contact with. By positioning the contest this way, Katy took the spotlight off herself and put it on her fans. She gave her fans permission to talk about the people that are most important to them.

The first runner-up in this contest was a pair of best friends from California who nominated each other as their Firework. Aurielle is hearing-impaired and Joel is blind, and they created a video about how important each of them had been to the other. They talked about being bullied when they were in school because of their impairments and how the other stood by them. Both Aurielle and Joel pour their hearts out in the video and explain how the other is their Firework. You can tell just how much these friends

BACKSTAGE PASS!

YOUR CUSTOMERS who are fans are probably already seeking to interact with other customers on behalf of your brand. You want to empower them to continue to promote your brand to other customers, but you also want to encourage them to relay the feedback they receive from other customers.

Here's a plan of action:

1. Create a list of fans that you want to connect with. It can be your entire list or a subset of that list. Consider your resources. If you've identified a total of 1,500 fans of your brand, and there's a two-person team handling this task, it will probably be a good idea to cull a subset that you can work with. If you do make a sublist, look for fans who are actively promoting your brand, especially those who are doing so online and via social media tools.

2. You want to connect with this group and empower the people in it to better promote your brand, but also to encourage them to give you as much feedback as possible from the customers they interact with. Think about the aspects of your brand and your products that you want to highlight, and make sure that your fans are careful to mention those points to other customers. You want to highlight aspects of your brand and your

continued...

products that you want them to mention, but you don't want to create "talking points" or scripted responses for them.

3. Keep in constant contact with your fans, and keep them in constant contact with one another. In the previous chapter's Backstage Pass, we talked about finding ways to connect your fans to one another, such as via a Facebook or LinkedIn Group. You want to find a way to bring your fans together, not only so that they can share the feedback they are getting in the field, but also so that they can play off one another's ideas. This means that they are more empowered to help your brand.

4. Give your fans at least one person who can be their contact within the brand. This is someone that they can get in touch with whenever they need to. For example, if a fan encounters a customer who is attacking the brand on a Facebook page, that fan may want to contact the brand directly to bring the attack to the brand's attention. This helps the brand address the feedback in a timely manner. It's important that the contact person knows to whom to pass along that feedback. For example, let's say you're the contact person for your brand's fans, and one of them alerts you to a technical question about the size of the belt used in a particular model of vacuum cleaner that your brand sells. In this case, you would need to get the necessary information from a product engineer who works with these vacuum cleaners, and relay the answer back to the customer.

One thing to keep in mind when working with your brand's fans (and this is another area where the lesson may seem counterintuitive at first) is to think about ways in which fans can help you other than by promoting your brand. Think of your fans as your eyes and ears out in the real world. Sure, they can promote your brand to other customers, but they can also address potential problems for your brand or relay negative feedback to you so that you can act on it.

love each other and how grateful they are to Katy for giving them the chance to share their stories.

What's absolutely brilliant about Katy's approach to this contest is that she took what could have been a strictly self-promotional vehicle and turned it into a way to *create something amazing for the people who love her.* She gave her biggest fans a way to tell the whole world about the most important people in their lives: their mothers, their fathers, their best friends, their favorite teachers. In the process, she became a little bit more important to them as well.

Remember that your brand's fans are special people who *want* to take control. They want to see your brand succeed, and they want you to tell them how they can help. Too many brands have the mindset that if the brand's customers are saying or doing things that reflect positively on the brand, it should leave them alone and not rock the boat. This is exactly the wrong thing to do! When you see your fans promoting you and acting on your behalf, you want to engage with them. You want to thank them and reach out to them because they want input from you. One time, I was in a meeting that a major brand was having with some of its fans, and one of those fans literally begged the brand executives in the room for a way to "help us help you!" Remember, your fans *want* to act in your brand's best interests, and they *want* you to tell them how to do that.

The following case study shows what can happen when your brand turns its marketing communications efforts over to its most passionate customers.

Fiskars Creates a Movement Based Around Its Most Passionate Customers

In 2005, Fiskars was facing a bit of a brand identity crisis. There was minimal online conversation about the brand or its products.

It hired the branding and identity agency Brains on Fire to help it better understand and benefit from what little conversation there was.

Fiskars discovered that its products, particularly its scissors, were popular among scrapbookers. In addition, Fiskars realized that most of the online hubs that were devoted to scrapbooking were very argumentative and not very welcoming to people who were new to the world of scrapbooking. In fact, many of the better-known scrapbookers were quite abrasive and were referred to as Scrap Bitches, a label that many wore as a badge of honor.

So here's what Fiskars had learned so far:

1. While there weren't a lot of conversations about the brand, there was a big online conversation about scrapbooking. And many scrapbookers were using Fiskars's signature orange-handled scissors and other crafting products in their projects.
2. Many of the online conversations about scrapbooking were a bit argumentative, and the environment wasn't very open to people who were new to the world of scrapbooking and ready to learn more about it.
3. Scrapbookers in general were much younger than Fiskars had assumed the customer base for its crafting products was.

The next thing Fiskars and Brains on Fire started doing was talking to scrapbookers individually. First, they started talking to the influencers in the scrapbooking space, trying to learn what they thought of the Fiskars brand. Next, they started talking to individual scrapbookers to learn more about their projects and about why they loved scrapbooking so much.

Perhaps the key takeaway for Fiskars from talking to scrapbookers was the revelation that these people weren't passionate about Fiskars's products, they were passionate about *what they could create* with Fiskars's products. For scrapbookers, their projects are very personal, often celebrating life milestones and the people in their lives who are most important to them. If a company produces a product that helps scrapbookers create better scrapbooking projects, then, by extension, that brand and its products become more important to these people.

With this key finding in mind, Fiskars decided to change its focus from trying to generate more conversations about its scissors to creating a place where scrapbookers could connect with one another. The brand realized that by creating a place where scrapbookers could connect and learn from one another, it would benefit because it had created something of value for its customers.

To build upon this point, recall that one of the takeaways for Fiskars in mining the online conversations concerning scrapbooking was the revelation that many of the online meeting places for scrapbookers could be quite abrasive and snippy. So Fiskars created a nurturing and welcoming environment for scrapbookers that would let them celebrate their love of scrapbooking. It created a blog where people who were passionate about scrapbooking could build a community. But here's the key: Fiskars didn't run the blog; it *turned it over to scrapbookers.* When Fiskars and Brains on Fire went across the country talking to scrapbookers, they did so to learn more about scrapbooking, but also to learn more about the scrapbookers themselves. Thus, when it came time to pick the scrapbookers who would blog for them, they had a good idea of where to start.

Fiskars wanted to create something bigger than a blog; it wanted to create a movement. To help with this, it gave its scrapbookers an identity: they were Fiskateers. Giving your fans an identity is critical because not only does it help to identify them as the special people they are, but it helps them connect with one another. Recall from the Introduction that Jewel has always had many fans, but only a few of her fans are EDAs, the hardcore fans who had loved her before the rest of the nation knew who she was. The Grateful Dead has Deadheads, a special group of devoted fans who pride themselves on having seen the band perform dozens of times.

One of my favorite sayings is, "A community is a group that has a *shared sense of ownership in something larger than itself.*" By giving these scrapbookers an identity as Fiskateers, Fiskars gave them a sense of ownership in the brand.

To extend that level of ownership, Fiskars asked four lead Fiskateers to run its blog (these Fiskateers are paid a part-time salary for doing this). It was careful to choose lead Fiskateers who weren't catty and abrasive and who would be more welcoming and helpful to other scrapbookers. The lead Fiskateers weren't just Fiskars bloggers; they were the leaders of the movement. If you wanted to become a Fiskateer, you had to go through one of the lead Fiskateers. That person had to get to know you, and you had to explain to him why you wanted to be a Fiskateer. Although there was an element of exclusivity, this resulted from the Fiskateers taking ownership in this movement. They didn't want to let everyone in, only those who shared their passion for scrapbooking and for one another, and who would work with them to help move the Fiskateers forward. In addition, when a person was accepted into the Fiskateers, she received a pair of limited-edition orange-handled Fiskars scissors with her personal Fiskateer number on it. This helped reinforce the exclusivity of membership and the members' ownership in the brand.

It's important to clarify something about the Fiskateers movement: it has a huge offline component. Many of the case studies featured in this book are focused on how brands have used social media to connect with their customers and fans online, but never forget the importance of connecting with your fans in a face-to-face setting. This is incredibly powerful. Many of the Fiskateers owned crafting stores or were regular customers of local crafting stores, so Fiskars worked to create ways to bring them together and connect them in a "real-life" setting. Sometimes it organized events just for Fiskateers. Other times, Fiskateers held crafting workshops in local crafting stores.

What Business Impact Has the Fiskateers Movement Had on the Fiskars Brand?

Here are some of the successes that the Fiskateers movement has accomplished, according to Brains on Fire (http://www.brainson-fire.com/work/view/fiskateers/):

★ Within 24 hours of opening the Fiskateers community, it reached its six-month goal for number of members.

★ There was a 600 percent increase in online conversations mentioning Fiskars by name in the first 20 weeks of the movement.

★ Stores that have had a visit from a lead Fiskateer experienced three times the sales growth of other comparable stores that had not hosted a lead Fiskateer.

★ Stores that have had a visit from a lead Fiskateer have seen their sales double as a result.

Note those last two bullet points. The Fiskateers movement is having a big impact on sales at the retail level. Again, the connections that you develop with your advocates shouldn't be locked into either an online or an offline setting. When you are trying to become more closely connected to your fans, don't forget the importance of connecting them to one another, both online and offline.

Note that Fiskars created a movement for its biggest fans and run by its biggest fans, then *got out of the way.* The growth of the Fiskateers blog and all the offline events are driven by the Fiskateers themselves. The Fiskateers movement continues to prosper because the Fiskateers have *a shared sense of ownership in something larger than themselves.* They feed off that sense of ownership, and they want the community to grow and create value for others. Recall in the Introduction the example of Jewel giving her EDAs ownership of creating the JewelStock concerts. Whether it's fans of a rock star or fans of a brand, these special people *want* to see their favorite rock star or brand succeed, and they will work hard to ensure that this happens.

Smart brands connect with their fans and give them the ability to connect with others on their behalf.

Pitney Bowes Creates a User Forum Where Customers Help One Another

If you have a question about or an issue with a product or service, the odds are that you will go to Google or another search engine and see if you can find an answer to your problem. Often, the top answers you'll get to your query will include results from online forums and message boards.

Pitney Bowes is a B2B company that specializes in creating communications products such as software and equipment for businesses of all sizes. The company also understands that its tech-savvy clients will often go to the Internet to get answers when they have a question about the company's products and services. With this in mind, Pitney Bowes created a User Forum that is designed to help customers with common (and not-so-common) questions and issues that they might have with its products (http://forums.pb.com/). The User Forum includes an area where customers can submit ideas on how to improve the existing products and services that Pitney Bowes offers, or suggest new ones.

The User Forum, as you might expect, often includes posts from customers with a question about or a problem with an existing Pitney Bowes product. Pitney Bowes actively monitors the User Forum for such posts, but it waits 24 hours before responding to this type of feedback from its customers. It does so partly because it wants to give itself time to properly research the problem, but also, more importantly, because the brand wants to give its customers the first chance at answering the question! By waiting, Pitney Bowes is giving its customers the chance to help one another, and it steps in only if it needs to do so. This gives Pitney Bowes's customers ownership of the forum and encourages them to take charge.

Not only does this help to increase customer satisfaction and loyalty, but the User Forum has a very real financial impact on the company. Pitney Bowes estimates that for every five visits to a particular question on the User Forum, one customer call to a call center is averted. Pitney Bowes uses an internal value of $10 per call, and in just one three-month period prior to 2010, Pitney Bowes estimates that it averted 30,000 calls. That's a cost savings of $300,000 over a 90-day period.

There is a major caveat to the idea of shifting control to your fans: you can't expect your fans to take ownership of a project or idea if they won't benefit from doing so—or, worse, if they will feel exploited in the process. This is a lesson that Moleskine learned the hard way when it tried to get its fans to crowdsource a new brand logo.

Moleskine Asks Its Fans to Create Its New Blog Logo, and Its Fans Fight Back

In 2011, when Moleskine decided to redesign its blog logo, the brand reached out to its fans to help with the project by holding a contest. Moleskine notebooks have always been very popular with the design community, so on the surface, Moleskine's holding a contest in which its fans (designers) would create its new blog logo seems like a good idea.

Moleskine called on its fans to design a new logo that would appear on its blog and its products. The winner would receive 5,000 British pounds, or roughly $7,500. The disconnect for Moleskine's fans was that while one lucky designer would get a cash prize for his or her hard work, the other entrants would go away empty-handed. By conducting the contest in this way, Moleskine was asking its biggest fans to literally invest thousands of hours of work in creating thousands of contest submissions, with only one fan receiving any type of compensation. Moleskine's fans felt that the brand was taking advantage of them, and they immediately began to voice their displeasure over the structure of the contest.

What could Moleskine have done differently to avoid this outcome? Designers, who make up a large portion of Moleskine's most passionate customers, didn't appreciate the brand's asking them to design a logo for free. The benefit to the brand was obvious, but only one designer would benefit from winning the contest.

One way Moleskine could have avoided this type of disconnect would have been to ensure that its customers' voice was represented within the company. For example, many companies have begun hiring community managers who serve many functions, one of which is to ensure that the voice of the community is represented when the company makes decisions like this. If Moleskine had had an online community manager, this person could have alerted the brand to the potential for a negative reaction to the contest from designers. Another option would have been to establish a brand advisory panel, a small group of Moleskine's most passionate customers that would advise the brand on how it should connect with its customers. If Moleskine had had a brand advisory panel, that panel would probably have advised the brand that the structure of the contest wouldn't be well received by designers.

So Why Don't More Brands Give Control to Their Fans?

Recall how The Donnas embraced what its fans were doing with thedonnasmedia.com. The band feels that it has a *trusting relationship* with its fans, which is why it sees this effort as something that helps the brand instead of hurting it. Yet your brand can't have a trusting relationship with its fans until both your brand and its fans understand each other.

For many brands, the thought of sharing control with their customers is pretty scary stuff. Brands have long embraced the traditional marketing model of broadcasting a message and staying on point with how you communicate to your customers. When social media tools such as Facebook and Twitter came along, many brands moved to these sites and adopted the same "push" model of messaging.

What's changed in the last 10 years or so is that your customers now have access to the same tools that you do, and many of them are more adept at using these tools than your brand is! Your customers as a whole can spread information, ideas, and opinions among themselves more quickly than you can reach them with your brand's message.

For example, a few years ago I was speaking at an event in Dallas. I was staying at the Sheraton downtown. At the airport, I found the shuttle that was running to the Sheraton downtown, which was about 10 minutes away. As we pulled away, the driver asked us *which* Sheraton downtown we were headed to. Apparently, there were *two* Sheratons in downtown Dallas, and I didn't know which one I was staying at! So I immediately jumped on Twitter and asked my followers which Sheraton downtown was hosting our event. Within two minutes, I had about five replies confirming the correct address for my hotel. And then I got a sixth reply from a friend who gave me the exact street address for my hotel *plus* the phone number. If I clicked on the phone number in the tweet I received, my phone would dial the hotel for me. After I arrived at my hotel and had settled in, I received a tweet from the Sheraton telling me that it had seen my tweet asking at which hotel the event was, but that it had also seen that several people had already given me the correct answer. Even though the Sheraton was closely monitoring Twitter and got back to me within half an hour, this was about 28 minutes after several members of my network had given me the exact information I needed.

Thanks in great part to recent changes in technology like social media and smartphones, your customers will always be more connected to one another than they are to you. Rock stars have always understood this, and they embrace it as a huge opportunity, not a challenge. Rock stars look for ways to better connect with their fans and to give them ownership of projects and messages that benefit them as well as the rock star. Smart companies like Fiskars understand this as well and are reaping the benefits of shifting control to their fans, whereas companies like Moleskine are still struggling to figure out how to truly understand their fans and stay connected to them. Your brand is probably also struggling with how to shift control to its fans and become more closely connected to them. I provide a framework for doing exactly that in the latter half of the book.

CHAPTER 3

Rock Stars Find the Bigger Idea Behind the Music They Create

One of the biggest challenges for companies is to create content and marketing communications that resonate with their intended audience. Many companies struggle to create content that engages its audience, and a main reason for this is that these companies aren't tapping into the bigger idea in the content that they create. When you focus on the bigger idea behind your products and services, you're focusing on the bigger picture that your products and services are a part of. When Graco created a blog about parenting, it found the bigger idea behind its content. When Fiskars built a brand ambassador movement that wasn't centered on its orange-handled scissors, but on what its fans were using those scissors for (scrapbooking), it found the bigger idea. In both these examples, the content created by these brands focuses on how and why people use their products, as well as their customers' lifestyles.

When you hear the marketing phrase "sell the benefit, not the product," this is the equivalent of tapping into the bigger idea behind your product. If Fiskars had decided to create a blogging community built around promoting orange-handled scissors, its results probably wouldn't have been as good. The scissors are a tool that helps create the scrapbooking project. Fiskars realized that it could sell more orange-handled scissors if it focused instead on the bigger idea, or why and how its customers were using those scissors.

Rock stars have always understood the value of creating music that taps into the bigger idea, themes that are powerful and that evoke an emotional response and connection. A perfect example of a rock star finding the bigger idea behind her music is the story of how Sarah McLachlan turned $15 into one of the most amazing music videos ever created.

Sarah McLachlan Helps More than One Million People with a $15 Music Video

In 2003, Arista artist Sarah McLachlan was preparing to create the video for her latest single, "World on Fire," when a newspaper article caught her attention. It was written by a Canadian university student named Mike Quinn, and it detailed the work he was doing with the charitable organization Engineers Without Borders (EWB). In his series, "Letters from the Field," Mike was explaining how EWB was acting to help areas around the world, and was telling the stories of some of the people he had encountered.

One of the people that Mike had met in the course of his work with EWB was a single mother in Ghana named Christy Yaa. In talking to Christy, Mike discovered that she was working two jobs for a total of 16 hours a day, 7 days a week. She was doing this to earn the $200 a year it cost to put her son through school. One of Christy's jobs was as an orange seller, and on a good night, she would sell 50 oranges at 2 cents apiece. Despite her meager earnings, Christy refused to take money from Mike when he attempted to buy oranges from her, and insisted that he take them for free.

Stories such as these touched Sarah, and she decided to use Mike's work with Engineers Without Borders as the focal point of the video for "World on Fire." So when Arista gave her a bud-get of $150,000 to shoot the video for the single, she didn't begin shooting; instead, Sarah gave away all of the $150,000 (except for $15) to 11 charitable organizations, including Engineers Without Borders. The funds allowed these organizations to perform work that touched and improved the lives of more than a million people around the world.

Now this was an incredibly generous gesture on Sarah's part, but in doing so, she had created a pretty big problem for herself: she now had to shoot a music video for "World on Fire" without any money! Actually, Sarah still had $15 left from the $150,000 that Arista had given her, so she took that money and bought a videocassette. Then she convinced a small team to donate its time to shoot the video and produce it.

Then she and her team got started on creating one of the most amazing music videos you will ever see. What Sarah did was explain in the video that the normal cost of the video would have been $150,000, and she used very basic slides to explain how that money was broken down into the individual expenses. For example, one slide explained that if the video had been shot in Los Angeles, it would have cost $200 each day for each production assistant. The next slide showed that the same $200 could be used to provide the school fees for 100 children in Ethiopia. Later, she explained how the $3,000 that was originally budgeted to cover catering for a one-day shoot in Los Angeles was instead spent on buying almost 11,000 meals for children living on the streets of Calcutta.

Throughout the video, Sarah explained exactly how the $150,000 would normally have been spent, expense by expense, but then, instead, told how the money was actually spent to help people around the world. And not only that, but throughout the course of the video for "World on Fire," she showed us the people that she had been able to help. We see people in Africa getting clean water because a well had been dug, or children liv-ing under a bridge getting a hot meal. The video is incredibly compelling, and it will inspire you one second and break your heart the next.

And it also got Sarah McLachlan a Grammy nomination in 2006 for Best Short Form Music Video. So for $15, Sarah was able to create a video for "World on Fire," touch and improve the lives of more than a million people, and garner a Grammy nomination. Not a bad return on a $15 investment. Additionally, one of those more than a million people around the world that Sarah was able to help was Mike Quinn's friend from Ghana, Christy Yaa. Ms. Yaa was given $1,000 of the money Sarah donated to provide a scholarship for her son's schooling, as well as a business grant for herself.

Sarah's video resonated with so many people because it spoke to themes and ideas that other people could connect with. If Sarah had created a video that was about her, it probably wouldn't have been nearly as popular. But by changing the video's focus to the themes of "World on Fire" and showing how actual people were being helped, it made it easier for us to connect with the song.

One of the areas where most brands constantly struggle when it comes to their online and social media marketing efforts is building engagement with the content they create. Whether it's on a blog, a Facebook page, or a Twitter account, most brands continue to look for ways to create more compelling content that actually holds the interest of and engages its audience.

In May 2012, Facebook did an internal study to determine what drives engagement on brand pages (http://facebook-studio.com/news/item/page-publishing-that-drives-engagement). It studied 23 brands across 6 different industries and found that all the content created by brands on their Facebook pages fell into one of three different buckets:

1. Updates promoting a product or service. For example: "Check out our 2013 model cars!"
2. Updates related to the brand. For example: "The thing I love best about getting a new car is _____ ."

3. Updates unrelated to the brand. For example: "TGIF! Is everyone ready for the weekend?"

Facebook also looked to see whether the brand's engagement goal was to generate shares, likes, or comments. Across the board, the study found that whether an update was related to the brand was the sole significant predictor of whether or not that update would generate engagement. In other words, Facebook found that its users were more likely to engage with content that was *related* to a brand than with content that was *about* the brand. This goes back to finding the bigger idea behind your content. Content that focuses on why your customers are buying your products and in what way they will use them is far more interesting to your intended audience.

For example, let's say that you don't own a digital camera, but you have decided that it's time to get one for those family trips you have planned for next summer. All you want is a small camera that you can carry in your purse or bag and that doesn't cost a fortune, but that will still let you take good pictures, even if you're not a professional photographer.

In doing your online research for cameras, you come across a blog that Nikon has set up. Which of these blog posts do you think would have more value for you?

1. "10 Reasons Why the Nikon Coolpix 2013 Is the Best Camera Money Can Buy!"
2. "10 Steps to Taking Perfect Outdoor Pictures with Any Camera"

Keep in mind that you're not in the market for a Nikon camera, you're in the market for an affordable camera that will take great pictures during your family vacation. The first post talks about the product, but the second post talks about how you will *use* the product. The second post addresses your core problem, which is, how do I take better outdoor pictures? Again, you need to sell the benefit, not the product.

Here's another example. Let's say your yard has become overrun with fire ants, so you decide to make a shopping run to try to find a product that will solve your problem. Your first stop is Home Depot, and you are greeted with a million different products, sprays, and chemicals claiming to kill every yard insect and pest under the sun. Since Lowe's is right down the street, you decide to go there as well to see if it has any different options. You find the lawn-care aisle, and you notice that there's a big crowd gathered there. You discover that, as luck would have it, Lowe's is holding a workshop on how to rid your lawn of 10 common pests, including fire ants! This is exactly the type of information you are looking for, and after listening to the expert's advice for 15 minutes, not only do you know exactly what product to buy to rid your lawn of fire ants, but you also learned that you can get rid of the flies in your house and the ants in your driveway with a couple of household products that you already own! Lowe's focused on teaching its customers how to solve their insect problems rather than simply trying to sell them products. In this scenario, Lowe's was focused on the bigger idea, and that ultimately did a better job of solving your fire ant problem.

HomeGoods Blog Focuses on Home Decorating, Not Home-Decorating Products

One of my favorite examples of focusing on the bigger idea behind your content is the HomeGoods Openhouse Blog (http://www.homegoods.com/blog/category/all/). The Openhouse blog doesn't focus on promoting HomeGoods home-decorating products; instead, it focuses on *discussing home decorating*. This subtle shift in the focus of the content makes it much more valuable to readers. If someone wants to get more information about HomeGoods's products, he or she can go to the company's website or its weekly circulars. By focusing its blog on home decorating, HomeGoods can accomplish three key content strategy goals:

1. Focusing on home decorating allows HomeGoods to create more engagement with its content. Most of the posts on the Openhouse blog have comments. As these readers engage with the Openhouse writers, they give these writers the opportunity to develop a relationship with the readers, which means that the readers will be more likely to become HomeGoods customers.

2. It allows HomeGoods to promote its products in the context of discussing home decorating. By taking this approach, HomeGoods can still promote its products, but not directly. For example, a writer could create a post about how to decorate the living room, and to illustrate her points, she could include pictures of a project that uses products from HomeGoods. If a commenter says, "Oh, I just love the throw rug in that picture! Does HomeGoods sell it?" that gives the Openhouse writer the chance to tell the commenter about the throw rug and say whether or not HomeGoods sells it.

3. Focusing on home decorating as the main topic on the Openhouse blog helps HomeGoods to establish its expertise in home decorating. This is a powerful selling point because we all want to buy from stores and brands that we trust. If the content that the writers create at the Openhouse blog makes us feel that the people at HomeGoods are experts at home decorating, it makes us far more likely to purchase home-decorating products from the brand.

★

As you might have guessed, I am a big believer in the power of teaching your customers rather than simply marketing to them.

Here are five ways in which teaching your customers can benefit your brand (and turn those customers into fans).

1. Teaching gives your brand a competitive advantage.

Your brand is probably operating in a marketplace with multiple direct competitors, and some of those competitors may have larger marketing budgets than your brand does. But if you teach your customers how to better use your products and how to solve their problems, that can help you stand out in a crowded marketplace.

Also keep in mind that when you teach someone something, you are empowering her. You are giving her a new skill or teaching her how to be better at something that she wants to kick ass at. If you can do this, you will earn her loyalty, and it will greatly increase the chances that she will advocate on behalf of your brand.

2. Teaching creates value.

Recall the earlier hypothetical example of being in the market for a digital camera. At the end of the day, you aren't interested in buying any particular brand of camera; you just want one that will take great pictures during your family vacations and that will be easy to pack when you are traveling. If your brand makes digital cameras and you can teach that customer how to take great pictures outdoors (especially of children playing), then you'll have created value and will probably earn that customer's business.

3. Teaching helps earn trust and loyalty and creates fans.

Let's be honest; it's hard for most of us to trust the average brand that markets to us. We tend to distrust most marketing that we come in contact with, because we assume that most marketers are looking out for their own best interests and simply trying to separate us from our money. But if you teach me how to get better at something that I am passionate about or help me solve a nagging problem, that gains my attention. Also, it shows me that you are trying to reach me with *my* best interests in mind. That helps you earn my trust and my loyalty. And going back to the first point, it's unexpected, so it helps your brand stand out.

4. Valuable content gets shared.

If your content creates value for me, I'm going to tell other people about it. On the other hand, if your content is focused on promoting your products, I probably won't share that content with anyone unless I know that he is in the market for that type of product. If your content is helpful and teaches me how to do something, I will be more willing to share it with others in the hope that they might learn from it as well.

Recall that one of the effects on Fiskars's business was that stores that had a visit from a lead Fiskateer experienced three times the sales growth of other comparable stores. The Fiskateers were teaching customers in these stores about scrapbooking, and that generated word of mouth about scrapbooking. Because the lead Fiskateer was teaching their customers, the stores that hosted a lead Fiskateer saw increased sales.

5. Sharing what you know means sharing your passion, and that inspires people.

When lead Fiskateers visit a crafting store, they are sharing their love and passion for scrapbooking. They are teaching others about scrapbooking, but they are also sharing stories about what scrapbooking means to them. We are drawn to stories from people who we can tell truly love what they do. We pay attention to these people because they are *sharing what's in their heart.* Teach what you know and share with us why you love what it is you do, and you may convince us to love it just as much.

Another way to find the bigger idea is to focus on ideas, themes, and beliefs that are relevant to your customers and that also pertain to your products and services. A good example of this is how Patagonia positions its blog, The Cleanest Line (http://www.the-cleanestline.com).

Patagonia Focuses Its Blog on Issues That Are Important to Its Customers

Patagonia's customers have always shared an interest in certain themes and beliefs, such as an appreciation for the environment, sustainability, and a love of the outdoors. When Patagonia decided to launch its corporate blog, The Cleanest Line, it decided that instead of focusing the content on its products, it would highlight the themes and topics that were important to its customers. As a result, you rarely find posts promoting Patagonia's clothing products; instead, posts about mountain climbing or efforts to protect an endangered coral reef are common. Patagonia creates content that focuses on the ideas and themes that are important to its customers.

In Chapter 1 we discussed how rock stars connect with their fans by being fans themselves. In much the same way, Patagonia shares many of the same passions as its customers. As Patagonia's bloggers write about the themes and topics that they are passionate about, they are also writing about the themes and topics that the company's customers are passionate about, because they share the same viewpoint. The great thing about this approach is that Patagonia can still promote its products, but it can do so in the context of increasing awareness of larger issues that resonate with its readers.

BACKSTAGE PASS!

FINDING THE BIGGER idea behind your content probably seems a lot more difficult than it actually is. This is very easy stuff, but it may seem hard because it's going to require you to look at the content you create in a new way, a customer-centric way.

To get started, ask yourself a couple of basic questions:

1. Who are your customers? Are they teenagers? Adults? Single moms in Minnesota? Start by thinking about who the people who buy your products are.

2. How are your customers using your products? What are they trying to accomplish? Another way to ask this question is, "Our customers buy our products because they want to _____," and then fill in the blank.

The point here is that you want to give some thought to who your customers are and how they are using your products. If you sell coffeemakers, why do customers buy your particular brand? Is it because they appreciate the fact that it can brew a pot of coffee 25 percent faster than most coffeemakers? If so, that suggests that saving time is a big consideration for your customers, which gives you valuable insights into their priorities and how they live their lives. So if the content you create focuses on helping your customers save even more time, it might resonate with them.

Here's another example: my friend D. J. Waldow did an interview on his blog, Social Butterfly Guy, with P. J. Hamel, an employee at the brand King Arthur Flour (http://socialbutter

continued...

flyguy.com/2012/02/22/video-king-arthur-flour-uses-face-book-to-build-friendships/). In the interview, P. J. talks about how King Arthur Flour uses its Facebook page as a sort of focus group with its customers. The brand often asks basic questions, such as what their favorite cooking magazine is or what the high temperature is where they live. Questions like these serve two important functions for brands like King Arthur Flour:

1. They give the brand valuable insights into who its customers are. Learning what its customers' favorite cooking magazine is gives the brand an idea of where its customers are getting their content. This can help King Arthur Flour in crafting its own content.

2. Asking your customers basic questions is a great way to build engagement and connections with them. For example, if a brand asks, "What's the high temperature going to be today where you live?," that might not seem very important. But it's a terribly easy question for customers to answer, and many will probably include *where they live* when they answer the question. In other words, a customer will probably say, "It's going to be 95 today here in Chicago." So King Arthur Flour can take all the answers it gets to this very basic question and actually get some solid insights into where its Facebook customers are located. The results that the brand gets from this question could influence how it crafts its content in the future. And besides, it's (nearly) free market research!

Notice that these examples continue to stress the importance of better understanding your customers. This is laying the groundwork to build those relationships with your customers that will ultimately lead to advocacy.

The CDC Uses Blogging to Raise Awareness of the Coming Zombie Apocalypse

Let's be honest, if you work for the CDC (Centers for Disease Control), creating content that raises awareness of the need to create an emergency/disaster preparedness kit is a tall order. Unfortunately, the need for an emergency/disaster kit isn't something that most of us think about until we or someone we know has been directly affected. In addition, many of us tend to procrastinate when it comes to planning or preparing ahead of time (I certainly do!). The CDC was given the task of creating content that raised awareness of a topic that probably isn't exactly top of mind for most of us.

So the CDC decided that instead of trying to get our attention about the need to prepare for a natural disaster, it would focus on the need to prepare for an *unnatural* disaster: a Zombie Apocalypse!

In May 2011, the CDC wrote a blog post detailing the need to prepare an emergency kit to help us survive the coming Zombie Apocalypse (http://blogs.cdc.gov/publichealthmatters/2011/05/preparedness-101-zombie-apocalypse/). The post was tongue-in-cheek, but the CDC's goal was to get people's attention, and then show them how to prepare an emergency kit should a natural disaster strike. The post walked people through exactly how to create an emergency kit in preparation for a zombie attack, but it also related how this same kit could help them if they were facing a very *real* disaster. Obviously, the CDC was using the Zombie Apocalypse as a hook to get people to pay attention to its core message.

And, boy, did it work! The post went viral, and as a result, the server for the CDC's blog crashed after more than 30,000 people visited the blog on the day of the post. At the time, the blog had been getting 3,000 visitors *weekly*. The CDC's Emergency account on Twitter (https://twitter.com/#!/CDCemergency) had 12,000 followers prior to the post's being published, but that number increased a hundredfold to *1.2 million* afterward, and a year later, in May 2012, it was at 1.3 million followers.

The CDC's use of the post warning of us the dangers of a Zombie Apocalypse did result in some criticism of the organization for taking a less than serious approach in trying to raise awareness of the need to prepare for very serious events. Personally, I thought the tactic was a great idea, and here are three reasons why:

1. It made the CDC seem more human. By displaying that it had a sense of humor (and a knowledge of pop culture), the CDC made itself a bit easier for the public to relate to. It made itself more accessible.

2. The CDC found a way to take a less than exciting message and make it interesting and fun. If the CDC had written a straightforward post on the process for creating an emergency preparedness kit, there would have been almost no chance that the post would have gone viral the way it did. People shared the post because it was crafted in a way that made it more interesting to the CDC's target audience.

3. Even though the Zombie Apocalypse was the hook, the CDC's core message still spread. This post raises awareness of the need to create an emergency kit, and now the topic is more front of mind for a greater number of people. So the end goal of the CDC in writing this post was achieved.

When you're trying to build awareness for a topic that isn't resonating as well as you would like it to, consider how you can link it to a more interesting topic or analogy, as the CDC did here. For example, for years I spoke and wrote about the value for brands of embracing and empowering their brand advocates and brand evangelists. This is a topic that I have been extremely passionate about for years, but I became frustrated because I noticed that most people didn't "get" the importance of this topic and share my passion for it. I wondered how I could better explain the idea so that it would resonate with others as it has with me. At the same time, I've always been enamored with how rock stars market themselves and connect with their fans. Then I realized that everyone understood how important a rock star's fans are to her. So I began using the Think Like a Rock

Star analogy to explain why this concept is so important to brands. I stopped talking about the importance of embracing and empowering brand advocates and brand evangelists, and started talking about how brands can turn their customers into fans just as rock stars have fans for their music. Suddenly, the idea resonated with others, and the proof is in the fact that you're reading these words right now. So if your idea isn't resonating with others, it might be that you need to change the way in which you present it.

So far, we've talked about how you can find the bigger idea behind your brand's products and services by creating content that teaches and that raises awareness of topics that your customers are passionate about. There's a third way you can tap into the bigger idea behind your content and marketing, and that's by creating content that's inspirational to your customers. To see how this can be done, let's look at how Red Bull is inspiring its customers by blending social media with traditional marketing in an online and offline approach.

Red Bull Inspires Its Customers to See How Far They Can Go

In 1988, Nike launched a new ad campaign featuring one of the most iconic slogans of all time: "Just Do It." The thrust of the campaign then and since has been to inspire people to be active, to engage in athletic activities. This is a classic example of a brand tapping into the bigger idea behind its marketing. Nike was smart enough to realize that its customers are people who want to be active. They are joggers; they hike; they run; they play. Nike celebrates their active lifestyles, and as a result of decades of branding, many of us feel that if we want to be active, we need to buy Nike footwear and apparel. By focusing on the bigger idea, Nike has made a powerful connection between itself and *how* people use its products.

Today, Red Bull is following a similar branding path, but with a different audience. Over the past decade or so, extreme sports have become very popular, helped in part by ESPN's coverage and exposure of the X Games. These games feature athletes performing stunts and racing in several different vehicles, such as motorbikes, rally cars, and skateboards. The events are truly a spectacle to watch, and it's quite exciting to see the athletes pushing and encouraging one another to best their score or time.

For the past 25 years, Red Bull has been aligning itself with these athletes and these events, sometimes via sponsorships, and other times by actually owning teams that compete in the events. Red Bull was smart enough to understand whom to target (primarily young and active males), and then to align itself with activities that this audience enjoys. Recall that in earlier chapters, we talked about how rock stars excel at creating something amazing for the people who love them. Red Bull is helping to facilitate events and activities that its customers enjoy. Its customers appreciate that it helps make extreme sporting events possible, and that helps convert those customers into die-hard fans. These fans understand that by its financial commitment to these athletes and events, Red Bull is helping to make them possible.

Red Bull's offline efforts to focus on the bigger idea behind its products carries over into its online and social media marketing. For example, as of May 2012, Red Bull's YouTube videos (http://www.youtube.com/user/redbull) had garnered a staggering 289 million combined views! The vast majority of the videos that Red Bull uploads aren't self-promotional; instead, they are focused on the athletes and the events that those athletes participate in. Even Red Bull's television commercials (which typically have several million views each) are focused on the athletes' accomplishments. The videos show the athletes performing incredible maneuvers and acrobatic feats, with the product itself taking a very secondary role. On the brand's Facebook page (https://www.facebook.com/redbull), the majority of the content is focused on the athletes and their accomplishments. Whether what it is offering is videos or pictures or questions, Red Bull wants the attention put on the athletes, not the product. And by the way, Red Bull's Facebook page is one of the most popular brand pages on the site, with more than 28 million likes.

By creating inspirational content that focuses on the athletes and their accomplishments rather than on the Red Bull product, the brand has found a way to engage and excite its customers and turn them into fans that love the brand.

But Remember That Your Fans Are Different

We've been discussing ways in which you can create more interesting content that's customer-centric, so that it helps turn your customers into fans of your brand, ways in which you can shift from creating product-centric content to creating content that focuses on how and why your customers use your products, and what's important to them.

But what if your customers are already fans of your brand? What type of content should you create then?

Your brand's fans see themselves as co-owners of your brand. They have a sense of ownership in the direction of your brand, and they want to see it succeed. Your fans are looking for more product-oriented details in the content you create. Think about a rock star's fans. They love the way the rock star taps into the bigger idea with her songs, but at the same time, they want a closer connection to her. They want to go backstage; they want to see her rehearse for a performance. They want special access. Your brand's fans want the same thing. They want more brand- and product-specific content. They already love your laptop, and they want to know what CPU you will be using. They want to see blog posts about how quickly Windows runs with an Intel versus an AMD processor. You should still consider how your fans are using your products and who they are when you are creating content, but don't be afraid to talk more about your products and your brand with your fans, because that's the type of content they want!

Three Ways to Create Better Content

We've discussed three different ways in which you can create more compelling content that will resonate with your customers and help turn them into fans of your brand. Let's review those three ways now.

1. Be a teacher.

Think about how your customers are using your product, and see if there's an opportunity to create content that teaches them how to use it better or to do a related task. The Fiskateers blog teaches readers how to create scrapbooking projects. The HomeGoods Openhouse blog teaches visitors about home decorating. Content that teaches readers a new skill to is very valuable, and it is content that is shared, which increases awareness of your brand!

2. Raise awareness.

Think about the ideas, news, and beliefs that are important to your customers, and create content that draws attention to these areas. Patagonia uses its blog not as a tool to promote its clothing products, but rather as a channel to discuss developments and news regarding the environment and the great outdoors. The CDC used a humorous blog post about the coming Zombie Apocalypse to draw attention to the need to create an emergency preparedness kit. Put the spotlight on the themes and ideas that are important to your customers, and your content will become more interesting to them.

3. Be inspirational.

Create content that inspires your customers to engage in a particular action. Red Bull's content marketing strategy is to create content that highlights extreme sports athletes and inspires others to take part in the same activities. As a result, Red Bull becomes more closely identified as the product that extreme sports athletes drink in order to perform their amazing stunts. Recall in the foreword that Kathy Sierra pointed out that rock stars want to make their fans *better*. Red Bull's content does this as well. It gives its customers the inspiration to become *better* at the activities that they love.

How Do You Find the Bigger Idea Behind Your Brand?

Collecting feedback is a great way to get better insights into how and why your customers are using your products. Here are a few ways in which you can collect valuable feedback from them that will help you find the bigger idea behind your content.

1. Amazon reviews.

If your product is sold by Amazon, pay close attention to the reviews it receives, because Amazon reviewers are great about explaining how they use the products they buy. For example, let's say that one of the products your company makes is in-ear earbuds. If you see multiple reviews that say something like, "I love these earbuds; my only complaint is that they often come out when I am jogging!" then you know that your customers are using your earbuds while they are jogging! This is significant if you are marketing your earbuds to college students, and it turns out that they are popular among joggers.

2. Company blog and/or customer support forums.

Check out feedback from your customers on either your blog or a customer support forum. Customers will often tell you if a product fails when they are performing a certain activity, or they might tell you that they love using your product while they are doing something else. Those activities that your customers are engaging in while they are using your product are clues to ways in which you can create more compelling content for your product.

3. E-mails, phone calls, and letters from customers.

Typically, customers will contact you either when they are having a problem with your product or when you have delighted them with it. In both cases, they can give you clues as to how they are using your product and what's important to them.

4. Talk to your customer support team.

This ties in with the previous point. Connect with the members of your customer support team and see what feedback your customers are giving them. What issues keep popping up repeatedly, and how are your customers using the product? For example, are the customers who complain that a particular model of laptop is getting too hot complaining about this happening only while they are playing online games?

With all of these suggestions, what you're looking for is trends in how your customers are using your product, and what's important to them. These clues can help you decide what type of content you should be creating that will be more valuable and relevant to them.

Now let's turn to the fourth reason why rock stars have fans instead of customers.

CHAPTER 4

Rock Stars Embrace and Empower Their Fans

When rock stars embrace their fans and give them ownership in helping them grow their brand, they show their fans that they trust them. Their fans appreciate that trust. It makes them feel greater attachment to the rock star. This devotion motivates fans to act in what they perceive to be the rock star's best interests—which often means promoting their favorite rock star to everyone they know.

We want your brand to become comfortable with the idea of connecting directly with its fans, so that both parties can benefit from that connection in much the same way that rock stars and their fans do. Rock stars embrace their fans to such an extent that they literally become fans of their fans.

Perhaps no rock star in the world does a better job of embracing her fans than Lady Gaga. Lady Gaga goes out of her way to communicate two very important messages to her fans:

1. You are special.
2. I love you.

That's it. By communicating this, Lady Gaga has attracted legions of fans worldwide. Let me share with you how she did it.

First, her fans are so special that they have their own identity. If you're a fan of Lady Gaga's, you won't be offended if I call you a Little Monster. That's the name and identity that Lady Gaga has given her fans. She also makes the famous "claw" symbol in her appearances and her videos. This symbol is recognizable to her Little Monsters, and it communicates that she loves them. It's a special bond between the artist and the people who love her the most.

Second, she often spotlights some of her fans at her concerts. She's been known to show them on the Jumbotron or call them on their phone during the concert. This communicates to them how special they are to her. And what a thrill to get a call from Lady Gaga! It also helps to reinforce to her fans the idea that *they* are the real rock stars.

Third, she communicates to her fans that she truly does appreciate them. As you might expect, whenever she has an in-store appearance or comes on a TV show, there are hundreds, if not thousands, of her fans standing in line to get a chance at seeing their favorite rock star. Lady Gaga is smart enough to realize how fortunate she is to have such devoted fans, and she will often send them pizza or hot chocolate while they are standing in line. What this does is remind her fans of why they love Lady Gaga. Imagine that you've been standing in line for three hours outside a Best Buy to see Lady Gaga, and you're getting hungry and irritable. Your stomach's growling, and just when you start to wonder if it's really worth it to keep standing in line, a crew member comes over, hands you a pizza, and tells you that it's compliments of Lady Gaga, who appreciates your standing in line to see her. Just like that, Lady Gaga probably made everyone in that line a fan for life. Plus, she would have validated to each of those fans the reason that they were standing in line for hours to see her. Lady Gaga communicated to those fans that she appreciates and loves every one of them.

There's one other thing that Lady Gaga does that makes her so successful: she's a *very* savvy marketer. Here's an example: in October 2011, Lady Gaga went on Twitter to ask her fans to help her promote her newest single, "Marry the Night." She told her fans that if they made the phrase "marry the night" the top-trending topic on Twitter, she'd reveal the cover image of the single. She added that this was earlier than her label wanted, but she loved her fans, and if they did what she asked, they'd get to see the single cover early. Her fans responded, and they were rewarded with a preview of the cover of "Marry the Night." Granted, Lady Gaga probably had full approval from her label to go ahead and release the single's cover. But by empowering her fans, she was rewarded with the additional exposure for "Marry the Night" on Twitter. Again, all this was possible because Lady Gaga loved and trusted her fans enough to embrace them and give them ownership in promoting her.

Note that Lady Gaga is saying thank you to her fans for behavior that they are already engaging in. She doesn't have to buy hot chocolate for her fans who are waiting out in the cold for an opportunity to meet her, but she does. She doesn't do it to keep them buying her products. She does it to show them that she appreciates the fact that they would stand outside in the cold for hours just to meet her. She's rewarding existing behavior instead of trying to provide incentives for new behavior.

Rewarding Existing Behavior Versus Providing Incentives for New Behavior

When you are thinking about how your brand can embrace its most dedicated customers, be careful not to focus on trying to encourage purchases. Your fans are already buying from you, so why spend time encouraging them to engage in behavior that they are already engaged in? It comes across as a disconnect and gives your fans a signal that you don't understand them. Instead, you want to find ways to reward their *existing* behavior *after* it occurs.

For example, if a car dealership runs a special every Thursday where female drivers get a $50 discount, that's not an example of embracing your fans. The goal of this promotion isn't to reward fans; it's to increase sales. Your intent should be to reward fans for behavior that they are *already engaging in,* not offering them a reward if they engage in a new behavior. Remember, you want to show your fans that you appreciate them, not that you will reward them if they buy more stuff. That's a loyalty program, and it's a completely different concept.

Here's another way of looking at it. Let's say you are into vintage video games, and every Friday, you visit Tom's Wayback Machine, a store that carries a wide variety of video games and other pieces of pop culture from the 1970s and 1980s. Occasionally you will pick up an item or two, but really, you go there just to look at all the wonderful items and maybe discuss with Tom, the owner, having had these trinkets as a kid. But next Friday when you stop by, Tom lets you know that he's running a special this month: if you buy $100 worth of merchandise, you'll get a 20 percent discount. When Tom makes this offer to you, he's not rewarding the fact that you stop by every Friday, he's trying to encourage you to make a larger purchase from his store. He's offering you an incentive to spend more. But let's try a different example. Next Friday when you come in, Tom greets you at the door and says, "Hey, I was hoping you'd come by today! I just bought a large collection of vintage video game cartridges, and I know you once said you wanted Super Mario Brothers 3 for your vintage Nintendo, so I put it aside for you. Here you are!" By doing this, Tom is rewarding your *existing* behavior. He knew that you wanted this video game because you had told him you were looking for it. Tom probably bought that large collection at such a good price that he could afford to give you this cartridge for free. The important point here is that Tom is rewarding the fact that you are a fan of his store. Offering you a discount for making a large purchase isn't an example of appreciating you as a fan. When you are attempting to show your fans that you appreciate them, the key question is this: who benefits more from your offer, your fans or your brand? There should be a direct benefit to your fans that is *not* tied to a purchase. Remember, if you want to cultivate fans, the goal is to reward existing behavior, not to attempt to provide incentives for sales. Fans are already giving you sales, so don't try to get more out of them. Instead, reward them with an amazing experience, and they will happily spend more.

But what about punch cards and other loyalty programs? This might be a program where if you purchase five drinks from a particular coffee shop, then your next drink is free. These offers do create loyalty, but that loyalty is typically more *to the offer itself* than it is to the brand. For example, let's say you are about to go to Starbucks to get a latte, when you remember that you have a Caribou Coffee punch card, and with your next purchase you will receive a free drink. This might be enough to encourage you to change your behavior for this purchase and go to Caribou Coffee instead of Starbucks. But what happens two weeks from now, after you've started a new punch card with Caribou Coffee? At that point, you know that purchasing a drink from Caribou Coffee won't earn you a free drink, so you may decide to go to Starbucks instead. Caribou Coffee was creating loyalty with you, but it was mostly loyalty to the offer, not to the brand. If you aren't sure if you are rewarding or providing incentives for behavior, ask yourself whether you are saying thank you for something that your brand's fans are already doing, or whether you are asking them to do something new. Offering a discount for purchasing more may seem like a reward, but it's really an incentive because it comes *before* the purchase. You want to look for ways to show appreciation to your fans *after* the purchase.

Blink-182 Finds Fans Stealing Its Music— and Rewards Them for It

Rock stars understand that their fans have their best interests in mind. They view their fans as special customers who want to see the rock star succeed and grow. A great example of this understanding happened in 2011 when the band Blink-182 was getting ready to release its first new single in eight years, "Up All Night." The band went on YouTube and discovered thousands of videos in which fans had used its music illegally. Typically, the videos featured fans either lip-synching the songs or performing skateboarding stunts or something similar to Blink-182's music.

After collecting and examining all the fan-created videos that had used Blink-182's music illegally, the band decided not to pursue legal action against its fans, but to reward them instead. It created a special music video for "Up All Night" that was composed entirely of scenes from the fan-created videos! The band went on to personally thank and highlight each fan at the end of the video. As you might expect, its fans' reaction to this move was overwhelmingly positive. The video currently has more than 700,000 views on YouTube (http://www.youtube.com/watch?feature=player_embedded&v=eabtzkY_jNs#!), and many of the fans featured in the video have created new videos letting their friends know how Blink-182 featured them in its music video.

From a legal standpoint, Blink-182 probably had every right to go after each and every one of these people on the grounds of copyright infringement. But the band was smart enough to realize that its fans weren't trying to hurt the band or its brand, they were actually helping to *promote* the band. So Blink-182 responded by embracing what its fans were doing and thanking them for it.

Now here's an important point: if Blink-182 had gone after these fans, it would very probably have created a backlash among the band's fans, and possibly even in the press. But because the band embraced its fans, those fans went on to create positive buzz about the band and probably expanded its fan base.

Remember, when it comes to the conversations that involve your brand, it's better to participate in those conversations than to attempt to control them. Notice too that in the Blink-182 example,

BACKSTAGE PASS!

ROCK STARS do a fabulous job of embracing and empowering their fans. Your brand can do this as well, and it is surprisingly easy. In many cases, a simple thank you goes a long way.

In previous Backstage Passes, we talked about how your brand should identify and begin connecting with its fans. You'll want to find a way to stay connected with this group, while at the same time being on the lookout for ways to connect with new fans. In many cases, this involves nothing more than simply reaching out to thank them for what they are already doing. Maybe a fan tweeted that she liked the service that she received from your store or wrote an update on Facebook that was a positive endorsement of your brand. By simply reaching out to fans like this and thanking them, not only are you rewarding their behavior, you are also encouraging them and other fans to engage in that same behavior.

In 2006, my blogger friend Chris Thilk wrote a blog post about how Universal was marketing its upcoming summer release *Miami Vice*. A marketing executive at the studio saw Chris's post and reached out to him directly, offering to chat on the phone to give him better insights into how Universal would market and promote the movie. From Universal's standpoint, this was a very smart move. The studio understood that Chris was, in effect, helping to promote the release of *Miami Vice*, so why not support that? By contacting Chris, Universal ensured that he had better and correct information; Chris, in turn, appreciated what Universal had done because it helped him write better blog posts. What happened next was pretty

continued...

interesting. Chris wrote a follow-up post telling his readers that Universal had reached out to him directly. That led to dozens of other marketing and advertising blogs writing about how smart it was for Universal to reach out to a blogger who was covering one of its movies. By reaching out to *one* blogger, Universal ended up getting great coverage for *Miami Vice* from many of the top marketing and advertising blogs—not a bad return on a 30-minute phone call to one blogger.

This is why I keep stressing that your brand shouldn't over-think social media marketing and connecting with your fans. Simply reaching out to your fans and thanking them for their support really *does* go a long way. After you have made a list of your brand's fans, do the following:

1. Actively monitor your fans' social media presence. Again, the issue of scale may come into play here, but you want to make sure that you are constantly keeping up with the content that your most passionate fans are creating. Simple Google Alerts can be put in place to notify you of new blog posts or content that your fans have created about your brand. You want to be aware of what your fans are doing.

2. Regularly thank your fans for being your fans. This seems like common sense, but trust me, most brands do not do this. And I'm not talking about a generic "We love you guys!" update on your Facebook page. I am talking about having your brand manager or social media manager e-mail or reach out to each fan and thank him. Again, you have to consider that you may not be able to stay in constant personal contact with all your fans (or perhaps not even a fraction of them), but you want to make the effort to do what you can.

3. Think about how you can empower your fans and benefit them at the same time. For example, if you see a fan of your brand blogging about your new commercial, e-mail that blogger and ask her if she is interested in doing an e-mail interview with the producer of the commercial. The odds are that the blogger will be thrilled by the opportunity to ask the producer a few questions and delighted that your brand would even think to ask. You have created value for your fan, and in return, that fan will create more positive content about your brand.

Remember, when you acknowledge your fans and make a sincere effort to communicate to them that you appreciate them, it *validates* their affection for you. It tells them that they are making the right choice by supporting your brand.

the band found a way to reward the *existing* behavior of its fans. This example ties in nicely with the case study from Chapter 2 of how The Donnas is working with its fans to share its music via thedonnasmedia.com. The Donnas understands that its fans want to share the band's music, so they've found a compromise with its fans that makes this possible. The band fully supports and encourages its fans to record and share live performances, but not music that's been released commercially. The Donnas' fans are totally cool with this, and they work with the band to make sure its wishes are respected.

Johnny Cash Goes to Jail Because That's Where His Fans Are

We've been looking at case studies of how modern artists have connected with and embraced their fans, but this concept isn't new. Rock stars have always tried to have a special connection with their fans. Let's look at how the Man in Black was doing this almost half a century ago.

In 1968, Johnny Cash's career was at a crossroads. He had been one of the brightest stars in country music a decade earlier, but after spending years battling his personal demons and drug abuse, he had seen his star dim. To his credit, by 1968, Johnny had gotten his feet back under him and was ready to revitalize his career. The problem was that not only had Johnny been out of the public eye for years, but musical styles had changed. Elvis Presley, Jerry Lee Lewis, and Johnny Cash were no longer what most music fans wanted to hear. Instead, it was all about the British invasion. The Beatles, the Rolling Stones, and Led Zeppelin were what music fans were clamoring for.

As Johnny started planning his comeback album, he understood that if his comeback was actually going to happen, his album had to be a hit. There was a lot riding on the success of the album, and Johnny understood that it might be his last chance to jump-start his musical career.

Johnny's persona as a singer had always been that of a man who's lived a rough life. He had a signature growl to his voice, and he often sang of his hard times and his brushes with the law. In 1955, he had recorded one of his biggest hits, "Folsom Prison Blues." The song became an anthem for inmates across the country. In fact, he often received fan mail from inmates, asking him to please come perform at their prisons. Johnny always embraced the fact that inmates loved his work, seeing it as a badge of honor. He frequently complied with their requests and performed at many prisons throughout his career.

So in 1968, needing to make a big splash, Johnny decided to perform a concert in a prison and record it as his next album. He settled on two possible venues: Folsom State Prison and San Quentin State Prison, both in California. He decided that he would perform at whichever prison accepted his offer first. Folsom beat San Quentin to the punch.

On January 13, 1968, Johnny arrived at Folsom State Prison for the concert. He understood that he wasn't performing for inmates, but rather for some of his biggest fans, who just happened to live in a jail. He embraced them, and it was almost as if he and his band saw giving them a stellar performance as a service. And that he did. From the start of the concert, Johnny poured his heart and soul into the songs, and the inmates were delighted. Johnny fed off the energy of the crowd, and the crowd fed off Johnny's performance. He played a set that was heavy on prison-themed songs, which were understandably among the inmates' favorite songs. Johnny closed his performance by playing a song written by an inmate at Folsom Prison, Glen Sherley. Johnny had first heard the song the night before, when the prison's pastor had played it for him. The song, "Greystone Chapel," touched Johnny, and he and his band immediately began rehearsing it so that they could perform it at the following day's concert.

Johnny literally risked his career on recording a concert album in Folsom State Prison, but the gamble paid off. *At Folsom Prison* was a commercial success and went on to be heralded by many music critics as one of the greatest rock albums ever recorded. The album went to number one on the country music charts in 1968, and the single "Folsom Prison Blues" from the concert went to number one on the country music charts and was the country music Single of the Year for 1968.

At Folsom Prison gave Johnny the hit album he was hoping for. It not only revitalized Cash's career but helped to extend it for another three decades. The reason why Cash is now viewed as one of the greatest rock stars of all time has a lot to do with the fact that he was willing to embrace his fans, even if he had to go to a prison to do so.

Another example of a rock star who does an excellent job of embracing her fans is Taylor Swift.

Taylor Swift Creates a Special Party for Her Biggest Fans

A hallmark of Taylor Swift concerts is the T-Party. Whenever Taylor performs at a concert venue, she creates a special spot in the arena where she and the other band members can unwind. This is a place where they can hang out as friends and chat, play video games, and just relax.

But this special spot serves a dual purpose for Taylor. During her performance, members of her staff will scan the audience. They are looking for about two dozen "special" fans, those who are most active and excited about the performance, or those who are wearing special outfits or have created signs for the event. During the concert, Taylor's staff will approach these fans and invite them to join Taylor and her band for a T-Party after the show. These fans will get to hang out, chat, and maybe even play video games with Taylor Swift. Obviously, these fans are over the moon with excitement at getting to spend some time with their favorite artist in such an intimate setting.

Taylor does this because she loves her fans and enjoys creating something amazing for them. For brand marketers, there are three very powerful business lessons that you can take away from the T-Party:

1. The T-Party gives Taylor the chance to have an intimate connection with *a very small group of her most passionate fans* and gives them an incentive to become even bigger fans. Let's say you are a Taylor Swift fan, and you're at one of her concerts when a woman approaches you. She identifies herself as Taylor Swift's mother, and says that Taylor would love to invite you to hang out with her after the show. By doing that, Taylor Swift just created a night that you will never forget. You probably just became a Taylor Swift fan for life, if you weren't one already. This means that not only will you probably be buy-

ing Taylor Swift merchandise for years to come, but you'll be encouraging your friends and family to do the same thing. Think about it: When someone does something for you, how do you react? You probably immediately think of ways in which you can do something for this person, ways in which you can *pay him back* for his generosity. How do Taylor's fans pay her back for including them in her T-Party? They pay her back by buying more of her stuff and telling their friends to do the same thing!

2. The T-Party lets Taylor connect with some of her biggest fans, but it also lets those fans *connect with one another.* That's incredibly powerful because Taylor is finding the people who love her the most and connecting them with one another, which is likely to help deepen their affinity for her.

3. The T-Party is one way Taylor rewards and thanks her fans for their *existing behavior.* This move deepens the love and affection that Taylor's fans have for the artist and validates their fandom.

Remember the story about Amanda Palmer giving a secret show for her fans in Boston? Her aim wasn't to generate sales (Amanda gave the tickets away). Her goal was to *create something amazing for the people who love her.* The key takeaway is this: both Taylor and Amanda created something amazing for their fans for free, but they will generate additional sales and promotion *as a result!*

Why do Taylor and Amanda have such passionate fans? In great part, it's because those fans know that Taylor and Amanda *love them.* They feel a connection with these rock stars, and that connection isn't based on a transactional foundation, it's based on an *emotional* one. Rock stars have always understood that connecting with their fans and developing an emotional relationship with them will *indirectly* lead to sales, whereas brands are focused on marketing efforts that *directly* lead to sales. Although both efforts lead to sales, it may be argued that the method that rock stars use cultivates more fans—and probably more sales as well.

You *know* this. You probably just aren't used to thinking about it in a marketing context. You know that people buy more of brands that they feel a positive connection with. You know that people buy more of brands that they feel appreciate their business. You know that saying thank you is appreciated.

What your brand probably isn't used to doing is developing a relationship and connection with your customers that then leads to sales. You want the sales up front; you want them to be a direct result of your marketing efforts. But if you follow the approach of rock stars and spend time cultivating a relationship and deep connection with your customers, not only will you get those sales, but you'll also see increased levels of customer satisfaction and loyalty. And this will translate into even more sales.

Remember, successful marketing isn't about cultivating sales; it's about cultivating advocates for your brand. Those advocates will drive more sales for your brand, and those additional sales will come from their efforts, not yours. Rock stars know that their ability to generate sales tomorrow will in great part be determined by how strongly they connect with their fans *today*.

And Now... the Obligatory Discussion About Apple and Its Fans

One of the key lessons we've been discussing so far has been the benefits that brands can enjoy if they connect with their biggest fans. We've been drawing parallels between how rock stars cultivate fans and how brands can do the same thing. We've mentioned that some brands are considered "rock star brands." Of these rock star brands, perhaps none has more fans than Apple. And curiously, Apple does very little to connect directly with its fans. It has almost no social media presence, and it has been purposely standoffish toward bloggers and the media. So if we are talking about the power of connecting with your brand's fans, how do we explain Apple's ability to cultivate its fans so easily?

While connecting with and embracing your fans is incredibly important, it's even more important to *understand* them. This was the genius of Steve Jobs. He understood what products his customers would want *tomorrow*. For example, in 1999, when Napster was at the height of its popularity, Jobs saw that the way people were sharing and storing music was changing and that customers wanted music in a digital form rather than on compact discs. So he started creating highly portable devices that would allow for the mass storage of digital music. Enter the iPod. Jobs also understood that most people who used Napster did so because they didn't want to pay $17.99 for a CD when they wanted only one or two songs. If there was a way to pay for an individual song, they would rather do that. Enter iTunes and the $0.99 digital song.

Steve Jobs had an innate ability to understand his customers and how they used his products. He knew what they wanted before they did. When did everyone decide that she wanted a smartphone with touch-screen scrolling? Five seconds after she saw Steve Jobs introduce the iPhone in 2007! The point is that the Apple example proves that while connecting with your fans is important, understanding them is even more so. And most brands need to focus on both understanding *and* connecting with their fans, because most brands don't have a visionary like Steve Jobs as the CEO.

Now before we move into the second portion of the book, let's review the four reasons why rock stars have fans instead of customers.

1. Rock stars are fans themselves.

By default, rock stars are part of the same group that they are trying to connect with—their fans. This means that not only do they have a greater understanding of who their fans are, but they have a vested interest in staying connected to them as well. Recall that in the Graco and Alamo Drafthouse examples, both brands are creating content and an experience that are consistent with what their customers want. Graco creates content that focuses on parenting for young parents with young children and allows its audience to create even more content. This ensures that Graco's point of view is the same as that of the customers it is trying to connect with, and it resonates more deeply with these customers as a result.

In the Alamo Drafthouse example, CEO Tim League is a huge fan of watching movies in theaters, so he goes out of his way to create an optimal viewing experience. This means that he removes customers who detract from the experience for the rest of his customers by causing distractions during the movie. If you are caught texting or talking on your phone in an Alamo Drafthouse theater, you will be asked to leave. This is a strict policy that the theater chain enforces, but it does so because the chain wants to create a great experience for its patrons. Alamo Drafthouse looks at this issue through the eyes of its customers, and attempts to create the viewing experience they want.

2. Rock stars look for ways to shift control to their fans.

Rock stars have always understood that some of the best marketing comes from a passionate fan to his friends. Think about it: Whom do you trust more, a friend who recommends a repairman when your kitchen faucet leaks or the commercial you see for Paul's Fix-a-Pipe? You trust your friend, and rock stars trust their fans, so they look for ways to shift control of their marketing messages to those fans. When Katy Perry wanted to create a video contest to promote her song "Firework," she asked her fans to talk about the people who are most important to them. And in the process, Katy became a bit more important to them.

In the Fiskars example, we saw that the brand embraced its biggest fans and empowered them to market for the brand as Fiskateers. The Fiskateers have their own blog, where they share their love of scrapbooking. They don't shill for the Fiskars brand, but they create content that resonates with other scrapbookers, and this leads to more positive exposure for Fiskars's products. By shifting control to its fans, Fiskars has created a much more effective marketing strategy.

3. Rock stars find the bigger idea behind the content they create.

Earlier in this chapter, we talked about how Taylor Swift connects with her fans at concerts. Obviously, Taylor also connects with her fans via her songs. Many of Taylor's songs are autobiographical, recalling her experiences as a teenager and young adult, so it should come as no surprise that Taylor is wildly popular with teenage girls! Teenage girls can relate to Taylor's songs because she is writing about many of the same life events that they are currently going through. Taylor has tapped into the bigger idea behind her music that makes it more relevant to her audience.

Recall how Red Bull positions its marketing. Red Bull has shifted its marketing strategy in recent years. It no longer focuses so much on its main product (an energy drink). Instead, it creates inspirational content that focuses on how people use its product. Red Bull's marketing showcases athletes performing amazing feats and participating in extreme sports. The marketing taps into the bigger idea behind why Red Bull's customers buy its product: because it will help them perform their activities at a higher level. Red Bull is focused on how and why its customers use its product, instead of being focused on the product itself.

4. Rock stars embrace and empower their fans.

Rock stars have always understood the value of connecting with and empowering their fans. By showing their fans that they appreciate them, rock stars cultivate deeper connections with their existing fans, who turn others on to the rock star, leading to even more fans. Additionally, passionate fans feel a sense of ownership of that rock star or brand. This gives fans a greater incentive to promote the brand or rock star to others and to act in what they believe is the brand or the rock star's best interest.

Don't Worry, I Know Why You Really Bought This Book

Sure, you want a rock star brand, but what you really want to do is *sell more stuff.* You're no different from rock stars in that regard. Sure, Taylor Swift and Lady Gaga and Amanda Palmer love their fans, but I'm betting that they also love the royalty checks they receive! Rock stars want to sell more stuff just as much as your brand does. They want to acquire new customers just as much as your brand does. Make no mistake about this.

The difference is that most rock stars and most brands travel very different paths to reach the same destination. The reason I am spending so much time discussing how and why rock stars focus on creating relationships with their fans is to help you understand that those relationships lead to rock stars being able to *sell more stuff.* Rock stars don't waste time crafting and beaming out marketing messages to people who don't want to hear them in an effort to acquire new customers. Instead, rock stars cultivate relationships with their biggest fans, which *indirectly* leads to their selling more stuff. These relationships with fans also indirectly lead to other awesome benefits, such as increased customer loyalty, improved product design, and more effective and efficient marketing.

By shifting your focus from cultivating sales to cultivating fans, you'll cultivate far greater sales as a result. But you won't cultivate fans unless you are creating *something of value for them.* Your fans want a deeper connection with you, their favorite brand. They want to know that you appreciate their efforts to help your brand succeed, and they want you to work with them to make sure that their voices and their input are heard and acted upon by your brand. They want to feel that your brand *understands* them. This is ultimately what your business wants as well, because by appreciating your fans and cultivating relationships with them, you'll realize the biggest impact on your revenue and your bottom line.

PART 2

UNDERSTANDING AND CONNECTING WITH YOUR FANS

CHAPTER 5

Who Your Fans Are and How You Can Connect with Them

We've been stressing the importance of not just connecting with your fans, but, more important, understanding them. There are two major reasons why this is so important:

1. You need to understand your fans so that you can understand what the nature of your relationship with them will be.
2. You need to understand *why* your fans love your brand.

When you communicate to your fans that you understand them, it validates their love of your brand.

Four Ways You Can Work with Your Fans

The rise of social media has played a big role in fueling the excitement of companies that want to connect with their fans and that see these social tools as an opportunity to help fans "tell our story for us." However, that's just one of four different ways you can work with your brand's fans.

share a
coke w/

1. Help your fans promote your brand.

This is the area that most brands focus their attention on when they look to connect with their fans. And for good reason, because fans *want* to promote your brand, and they are already doing so. Your fans are constantly looking for opportunities to promote your brand to other customers, because they want to see other people become fans of your brand, too.

What is it about your brand that you want your fans to stress to other customers when they talk to them? Are there features on your new product that you feel make it vastly superior to the competition? Is your product created from 100 percent recycled products? Whatever those features are, make sure your fans understand that you want to make other customers aware of them.

2. Help your fans generate more sales for your brand.

As a natural extension of promoting your brand to other customers, your fans will no doubt have plenty of chances to "close the sale" with other customers. Think about what you can offer your fans to help them convince other customers to try your product. Maker's Mark gives its ambassadors stickers to put on their receipts when they eat in restaurants. If the restaurant served Maker's Mark, they put a sticker on the receipt thanking it for doing so. If it didn't serve Maker's Mark, they put a sticker on the receipt asking it to please start.

Your fans are going to be in constant contact with others and singing your brand's praises to them. Give those fans the tools to close the sale with potential new customers.

3. Help your fans provide customer service for your brand.

This is something that your fans are already doing for your brand, so it pays to help them do a better job of it. Encourage your fans to be your eyes and ears, especially on social media sites, to help bring potential customer service issues to your attention. Again, this is where it pays to let your fans have someone at your brand that they can reach out to at all times. Also, remember that if your fans can solve a customer service complaint for a customer or answer a question, that potentially removes the need for that customer to call or e-mail you about the issue. This results in a cost savings for your brand.

4. Let your fans become a feedback channel for your brand.

This is probably the most undervalued role that your fans can play for your brand. You want to constantly encourage your fans to give you as much feedback as possible on the interactions they are having with current and potential customers. Ask your fans to tell you what they are hearing about the things that other customers like about your brand and the things that they dislike. Ask them for the same type of feedback about your competitors. Also, ask your fans to pay close attention to the reasons why some customers say they bought your product and the reasons why others say that they did *not*.

You also want to remind your fans that how they interact with other customers will reflect positively or negatively on your brand. For better or worse, other customers will view your fans as being an extension of your brand. So you want to especially stress to your fans that they should be mindful of the tone of voice they use when they are communicating with other customers. For example, your fans are passionate about your brand, and they are likely to want to defend it to other customers. But if a fan gets into an argument with another customer about your brand, that could reflect negatively on your brand. Always remind your fans that if they aren't sure how to respond to another customer, they can contact your brand and you'll be happy to help them. We'll talk about this more in the next chapter.

And Now, a Word About Crowdsourcing

A few years ago, brand marketers started getting excited about the idea of letting customers crowdsource part of their marketing, such as their commercials or logos. At first blush, the idea seems like a win-win. The brand benefits because its customers are creating its marketing for it, and the customers win because they get a say in the brand's marketing efforts.

But here's the problem: if you give everyone a say in your marketing and promotional efforts, you typically end up with a bland message that doesn't really resonate with anyone. There are many different reasons why fans might love your brand. If you took four of your fans, each of whom loves your brand for a different reason, and let them design a commercial for your brand, what would happen? Each of the four would want to highlight the particular reasons why he loves your brand, which means that the finished product would probably be a convoluted mess with no real focus or message.

So remember that just because you can give your customers a say in your marketing and promotional efforts doesn't mean you should. It's far more important for you to really *understand* your fans than it is to not understand them, but then use them to crowdsource ideas for you.

Understand Why *Your* Fans Love *Your* Brand

In the previous chapter, we talked about how Lady Gaga connects with her fans, and how she gave them a special identity: her Little Monsters. Lady Gaga began calling her fans Little Monsters or Monsters when she saw how they reacted every time she performed the song "Bad Romance" during her Monster Ball tour. They would get very raucous and start screaming, so she asked them to calm down because they were acting like Little Monsters! Thus, the identity was born. Now it's a badge of honor for Lady Gaga's fans, and they greet one another by making the claw/paw sign that Lady Gaga made during the music video for "Bad Romance."

Just as Lady Gaga did with her fans, you need to figure out what the special identity is for your brand's fans. Not all of your fans love your brand for the same reason. You need to figure out what it is about your brand that attracts fans. For example, in 2010 and 2011, when I worked with Dell to help facilitate its Dell Customer Advisory Panel (CAP) meetings with its fans, I was struck by the different reasons why the fans attended loved Dell. Some of the fans loved the Alienware product line; others were fans of Inspiron laptops. One fan loved how easily the products could be customized online; another loved the solutions that Dell offered to the enterprise space. Personally, I am a big fan of Dell because I'm friends with many of the people who run Dell's social media efforts, and I know what good work they are doing. The point is, even in a room of only 15 or so fans, there were several different potential reasons why those people were fans of Dell.

Melody Overton is known as Starbucks Melody on the web. She is a huge fan of Starbucks, and she even has a blog devoted to her love of the brand (http://www.starbucksmelody.com/). I talked to Melody about why people are so devoted to the Starbucks brand because I wanted to learn more about what the "identity" was for the brand's fans. "I think that people become passionate about Starbucks for a variety of reasons," Overton explained. "For some people, the stores really represent that place where they've connected with family, friends, small groups, and so they have these very positive associations with Starbucks. It is that 'third place' effect that Starbucks is famous for. And some customers really are able to see that Starbucks can use its large size to do good things, both locally and globally. And, of course, lots of people just like the coffee and get very passionate about 'their drink.'" Just looking at

Melody's answer here, we have three possible reasons why people are fans of Starbucks:

1. They love their drinks.
2. They love the idea of the "third place" effect.
3. They love the way Starbucks can use its size to do good things for people, both locally and globally.

So there are three possible identities or reasons why Starbucks has fans. If you work for Starbucks and you want to create a program designed to connect with the brand's fans, you need to understand these different reasons why some of your customers are fans of your brand.

Think of it as trying to find the one common thread that runs through your fans. It could be that your brand has different groups of fans who love it for different reasons, as we saw in Melody's quote. In the Dell example, the company may have one fan community built around its Alienware product line and another built around its Inspiron product line. But its Alienware fans are hardcore gamers, for the most part, so the fans of the Inspiron brand might be fans of that product line for a completely different set of reasons from those motivating the fans of the Alienware product line. The two groups love the brand for different reasons, and if you attempt to connect with both groups on the same terms and in the same context, your efforts won't resonate equally.

This leads to another important lesson about cultivating fans of your brand: fans support brands that they feel understand them. Your fans want to feel understood; they want to know that you *get* them. This is why I've been stressing that it's more important for you to understand your fans than it is for you to connect with them. As we discussed in the previous chapter, other brands make far more of an effort to connect with their fans than Apple does, but few brands understand their fans as well as Apple. That's the difference; you can be connected to your fans, but if you don't

BACKSTAGE PASS!

IN THE BACKSTAGE PASSES for the previous chapters, we started outlining the process that your brand can take to begin identifying and directly connecting with your fans. To tie in with the lessons from this chapter, we want to add a new layer to this process: begin by identifying *why* each customer is a fan of your brand. As you reach out to and thank each fan, start trying to figure out why she loves your brand. Sometimes she'll tell you without your having to ask, but if she doesn't tell you, ask her!

Here's why this is important: it's adding another layer to your understanding of who your fans are and why they advocate on your behalf. When you interact with your fans, try to determine why it is that they love your brand. Maybe it's a particular product line they love, maybe it's the customer service they get at the retail level, or maybe it's your company's efforts to go green. Whatever the reason, once you start to identify why your fans love you, you can begin to get a better insight into who your fans are. For example, suppose you start talking to your fans and you learn that 45 percent of them love your brand because your products are made with completely biodegradable materials. Knowing this could have a significant impact on your future marketing, couldn't it? This information gives you a better idea not only of who your fans are but of the best way to connect with them.

The better you understand your fans, the better you can connect with them and the more likely they are to advocate on your behalf.

understand who they are and why they love your brand, that connection won't be as strong as it could be.

So how do you figure out your fans' identity? In Chapter 3, we discussed focusing on the bigger idea behind your marketing and communications. That applies here as well. You want to think about how your product fits into the lives of your customers.

Don't limit your thinking by focusing just on your product. Go beyond that. Think about how your customers are *using* your product, and to what end. Look online at product reviews, and watch for comments from your fans that say, "I love Brand A because..." The reason your customers give for loving your brand is typically a big clue to their identity. Some examples could include:

I love Brand A because... it uses biodegradable materials in its products.

I love Brand A because... its products all work together seamlessly, allowing me to be more productive.

I love Brand A because... every time I visit one of its stores, I am immediately greeted by a smiling employee who genuinely wants to help me.

Once you figure out what your fans love about your brand, then you can better build a lasting relationship with them.

Influencers Versus Fans: Which Is Better for Your Brand?

In recent years, thanks in large part to services like Klout and Kred that measure online influence, brands have been scrambling to connect with influencers. And for good reason: if someone is influential about a topic associated with your brand or is viewed as an expert in that space, then that person could expose your brand to an entirely new audience if he promotes it. If this person has also built a large following on social media sites, that just means more potential exposure for your brand.

But is it more effective to reach out to influencers or to your fans? In order to answer this question effectively, you need to do two things:

1. Understand the difference between influencers and fans and what motivates them.
2. Understand why you want to reach out to either group.

First, let's consider the difference between an influencer and a fan of your brand. Let's say your brand makes exercise equipment, and it is about to roll out a new weight-training device. You want to build awareness of this new product, and you can reach out to two different people to help you promote it, Amy and Nick. Nick is a fitness blogger; he has 50,000 followers on Twitter, 75,000 people read his blog every month, and Klout identifies him as being very influential in the areas of fitness and healthy living. On average, Nick reviews three weight-training products or diet supplements on his blog each week. He has never blogged about your brand or its products before.

The other person you are considering reaching out to is Amy. Amy has a much smaller following on Twitter (roughly 1,500 people), and her blog averages a few thousand visitors a month. She isn't viewed as being a fitness blogger; although she does occasionally blog about fitness and healthy living, her blog is mostly about her life as a college sophomore and all that it entails. But Amy also happens to be a *huge* fan of your brand. She doesn't blog about fitness very often, but when she does, she often mentions your brand and its products.

So if you could reach out only to either Nick or Amy to help promote your brand's new product and build awareness for it, which should you reach out to? There are specific advantages and disadvantages to going either route. If you reach out to Nick, you're connecting with someone who has a wide reach and who is viewed as an expert in the fitness and healthy living category. So what Nick says matters to a lot of people who are potential customers for this product. The downside is, Nick probably doesn't have much affinity for your brand, and he moves on quickly. He's constantly reviewing exercise equipment, and the fact that he's never reviewed one of your products is a bit worrisome. In addition, if he reviews your product and hates it, then you've just turned off the very audience you were trying to connect with. Of course, if Nick reviews your product and loves it, that's great exposure for it, but again, he'll quickly move on to another product review, so even if you get great exposure from Nick, it's probably not going to last very long.

Now let's look at connecting with Amy. Amy doesn't have the reach that Nick does, and she isn't viewed as an expert in the fitness space. But the big advantage of connecting with Amy is that she's already a passionate fan of your brand. This means that Amy has a big incentive to promote your product to her friends and to see it do well. So if Amy loves your product, she will blog about it today, and probably tomorrow as well. Granted, she doesn't have anywhere near as large a network to connect with as Nick does, but it could be argued that although her network is much smaller, she actually has more influence over it. Nick's readers come from all over the globe, and he's probably never met or talked to the vast majority of them. They probably don't have a personal connection with him. But even though Amy's network is only a fraction the size of Nick's, it's made up of people she has a very personal connection with: her friends, her family, and probably her college classmates. So just as Nick can influence his audience by being viewed as an expert, Amy can influence her audience because she knows its members personally.

So which group should you reach out to in order to promote a new product: your fans or influencers? We need to go back to *why* you would want to reach out to either group. If you want to generate short-term buzz and excitement, an influencer outreach program can often achieve this. On the other hand, connecting with your fans benefits your brand today and tomorrow for many reasons that we've been talking about so far in this book. Thus, the benefits of connecting with your fans are obviously longer-term.

Of course, there is another option: you could connect with influencers that are also fans of your brand! We've touched on this a bit in previous chapters, but this is another advantage to connecting with and understanding the fans of your brand as individuals. Sure, it takes a bit more time and research, but it's worth it.

For example, a few years ago Pepsi launched an influencer outreach campaign dubbed the Pepsi 25. The brand was rolling out a new logo, and in order to help generate buzz for that logo, it sent packages to 25 online influencers. I was asked to participate in this program, and I received three packages from Pepsi. The first two packages were filled with several empty Pepsi cans, each can showing a different logo from Pepsi's past. It was a nice way to see the evolution of the brand's logo. The third package included six cans of Pepsi with its new logo (this happened in 2008). Also, I was given a form letter explaining that I was one of the first 25 people to see Pepsi's new logo.

This campaign didn't really resonate with me for several reasons, but perhaps the biggest reason why this campaign was a disconnect for me was that *I am a huge Dr. Pepper fan*! So Pepsi had two strikes against it by putting these self-promotional packages in the hands of someone who not only doesn't like its product, but is a fan of one of its competitors. Yet as I was reading the information that Pepsi sent me, I was struck by how the brand emphasized that I was one of the first people to see the "new look" for Pepsi's brand. Honestly, that really didn't matter to me, because I'm not a fan of Pepsi. But what if Pepsi had put these packages into the hands of one of its biggest fans? If I had been a true fan of Pepsi, and I had received these packages with the explanation that I was one of the first people in the world to see the brand's new logo, I would have been over the moon with excitement! So the lesson here is that while it's sometimes a good idea to reach out to influencers, it's always a good idea to *understand* whom you want to connect with, so that you'll know whether the people you are reaching out to are a good fit for what you want to accomplish.

How Do You Create a Killer Influencer or Fan Outreach Program?

Since we are talking about what does (and does not) make an effective outreach program, let's go ahead and list the steps involved in crafting a successful effort.

1. Figure out why you need to do an outreach program to begin with.

Typically, an outreach program is designed to build awareness of a new product or a new service, or even of a new partnership. If you want to use an outreach program to build awareness, you need to figure out what it is you want to build awareness of, and that will help you determine whether an outreach program is the right path for you to take.

2. Define what will make the outreach program a success.

Whenever I talk to clients about launching an outreach program, or really anything that is social media–related, I tell them to complete this statement: this effort will be a success if X happens. Figure out what the X is for your outreach program. For example, it could be a 10 percent increase in positive product mentions online, or it could be a 15 percent increase in product trial sign-ups. But before you completely craft and launch the outreach, you need to determine what will need to happen in order for it to be a success. What are you trying to accomplish? Figure this out and make sure that what you are measuring ties back to that goal. For example, if the end goal of your outreach is to increase product sales by 15 percent, why would you measure how many additional Twitter followers you gained? You shouldn't, unless you know how gaining Twitter followers affects product sales. We'll talk about this more in later chapters, but when you are measuring the success of any social media marketing effort, measure engagement only *if* an increased level of engagement can be tied directly to your goals for the program or campaign. Too many brands fool themselves into believing that their social media efforts are successful simply because they have increased levels of engagement. An increased level of engagement *is* often a good thing, but you need to do the research to understand how getting more engagement via social media will ultimately lead you to your goals for the program.

3. Do your research and figure out exactly whom you should be reaching out to.

Crafting a list of viable outreach candidates will require a lot of research and legwork on your part, but the extra work will pay off and will increase your chances of having a successful program. Yes, it means that you will have to spend more time doing a sort of background check on the people you think you want to reach out to, but it also increases the chances that your program will be successful because it helps ensure that you will be reaching out only to people who are *interested in your program.* This is not a step you want to cut corners on. The good news is, if you have been doing the work outlined in the Backstage Passes I've included in the previous chapters, you may already have a few viable candidates for your outreach program among the existing fans that you are already (hopefully) connecting with. So that's a perfect starting point for your brand.

4. Make sure your pitch is relevant to the people you are reaching out to.

Think about what it is that you want to build awareness for, and also think carefully about *why anyone else would care*. Before you contact someone as part of an outreach program, always ask yourself, "Why will this be interesting to this person?" In order to get an influencer or even a fan to promote you as part of your outreach, you need to make a *relevant* pitch to her. Remember, you are asking this person to positively promote your product or service to others. In order to make that happen, you need to give her something that she values. It could be relevant content or a desirable product. But first you have to create value for the person you are trying to connect with, in order to get her to promote you to her network.

Here's an example of how to create a relevant pitch. A few years ago, Kaitlyn Wilkins contacted me as part of a blogger outreach program she was doing. Kaitlyn was working for Ogilvy PR, and one of Ogilvy's clients was Ford. Ford's CMO, Jim Farley, was appearing at an auto show, so Kaitlyn reached out to a few marketing bloggers with this idea: if we wanted to submit a question to Jim, Kaitlyn would have Jim answer our questions for us, in the form of a video. She created a video that featured the questions from about five different marketing bloggers (including me), and Jim answered each question during the video. The pitch itself was excellent because Kaitlyn understood that this would be content that we marketing bloggers would find value in. And speaking of value, the question I asked Jim was, "Are there any areas that Ford can point to where social media has either lowered business costs or improved existing processes?" Jim gave a fabulous answer, revealing that social media had led to *massive* cost savings for Ford. Jim detailed exactly how using social media for one campaign had greatly reduced the amount that the automaker had had to spend on traditional advertising. I was thrilled with his answer, and I wrote a blog post chronicling it, as well as how Kaitlyn had crafted this outreach effort. To this day, that one blog post remains one of the most popular blog posts I have ever written, but it all came about because Kaitlyn was smart enough to craft her pitch so that it would provide value for the bloggers she reached out to. I got a chance to create great content with the CMO of Ford answering my question, and Ford got great exposure on my blog and continues to do so to this day. As an added bonus, Kaitlyn also got great exposure because I focused on what an amazing job she had done with the outreach. Come to think of it, Ford and Kaitlyn are still getting exposure here in this book, aren't they? See what can happen when you craft a relevant pitch for your outreach program?

5. Be responsive and available.

Whether you are sending a pitch to a blogger on a story idea involving your brand or sending 10 fans your new model digital music player, you want to be available to these people. You want to be able to address any issues, questions, or concerns that they may have. For example, if you are pitching a blogger on writing a story about your new model of digital music player, you want to answer any technical questions that the blogger may have in a timely manner, because this could determine whether or not he will blog about your device. Remember, whether you are reaching out to a fan, an influencer, or someone else, he will be doing you a favor if he promotes your brand's product. So act accordingly.

6. Make it easier for your audience to promote your product or write about your story.

Again, if you reach out to a blogger or influencer and ask her to cover your story or use your product, you are asking her to *do you a favor*. So if you want a blogger or influencer to participate in your outreach program or blog about your story, you need to make it easy for her to do so. For example, if you want to encourage a blogger to write about how effectively your brand is using social media to connect with realtors in Southern Arizona, you need to be ready to show (and explain) some actual numbers from those efforts. Asking me to blog about how your client has seen "big gains from using social media marketing" isn't very compelling, but if you can show me that your client can attribute a 28 percent growth in sales over the last six months strictly to using Twitter, that will get my attention.

Also, make your pitch shareable. If you want me to promote a white paper to my network, make it easy for me to do so. Create a custom tweet for me and include it in the e-mail pitch. For instance, "Local bakery sees 28% growth in sales since January from using Twitter—http://www.url.com." Remember that whoever you are pitching is just as time-starved as you are. People have too much on their plate (just as you do), and you need to make it as easy as possible for them to cover your story. If you can show them quickly how your story idea will create value for them and their network, your chances of getting coverage increase dramatically.

7. If your outreach involves giving fans or influencers a product, remind them of the proper disclosures.

In short, whenever they discuss it or create content about it, they need to disclose that they received the product from your brand, along with any other forms of compensation you might have given them. But check to make sure that all the relevant disclosures for your particular product and industry are covered.

8. If your outreach involves giving fans or influencers a product, include some way in which they can handle referrals.

For example, if you give a fan your new model vacuum cleaner, when he is showing his friends how amazingly well it cleans his carpets, how can that fan move his friends closer to a sale? Maybe you could give him the contact information for someone at your brand that he could reach out to, or simply a 25 percent off coupon. The point is, if you are putting this product in the hands of some of your best salespeople, give them the tools to help close the sale!

9. If your outreach involves giving fans or influencers a product, create a way for those people to connect with one another.

A few years ago, I was involved in a blogger outreach campaign for a very nice digital camera. The pool of bloggers that received the camera included a nice mix of marketing bloggers, lifestyle bloggers, and photography bloggers. But when I got this amazing camera, I took crappy pictures with it because I had no idea how to use it! In the hands of a seasoned photographer, this tool could have created wonderful pictures, but in my hands, it took blurry disasters. I would have loved to have been able to go to a site or blog where I could have connected with the other bloggers involved in this outreach and asked them for advice on how to better use this camera. Think about how you can connect the people involved in your outreach to one another because this will also be a very valuable *source of feedback for your brand.* If this brand had created a site for the members of this outreach, it might have seen that several of us loved the camera, but were overwhelmed by its many features and didn't know how to use it to reach its full potential. That's very important product feedback that this brand could have acted on.

10. Think of your outreach as the beginning of a relationship with its participants, not as a campaign.

Even if you are reaching out to influencers, there's no reason why they can't become fans of your brand, right? Don't just send out your product and wait for them to write a blog post that (hopefully!) is glowingly positive. Actually take the time to reach out to each of them and not only ask her honest opinion about the product, but try to find a way to keep working with her. Maybe this particular product didn't work for one particular influencer, for whatever reason. Talk to these people and try to figure out what would have made the outreach and the product work better for them. Remember, we as customers love responsive brands! We want to know that brands appreciate our feedback, and that they are willing to act on it. Take the time to acknowledge and act on the influencers' opinions, and you may just convert a few of them into fans of your brand.

Relax and Breathe Deeply; This *Will* Get Easier

We've covered a lot of ground in this chapter, and we'll cover even more in the next one. So don't beat yourself up if this seems a bit overwhelming or like too much to take in all at once. Just remember that your efforts should always go back to this one simple question: How is this going to directly benefit your brand's fans? If you are creating value for your fans, then you've won. So even if some of this doesn't make complete sense at first, just trust that as long as you are acting in the best interests of your fans, *your brand will benefit*. Rock stars have always understood this: They embrace and support their fans, knowing that their fans will embrace and support them right back.

CHAPTER 6

How to Handle Negative Comments and Convert Angry Customers into Passionate Fans

In Chapter 1, we explored the idea that *participating in a conversation changes that conversation.* This point is lost on many companies when it comes to what their customers are saying about them online, especially if it involves negative comments and feedback. Many companies have the mindset that "if we ignore it, it will go away." This is a shame because directly interacting with customers who leave negative feedback online is often the quickest way to convert those customers into fans of your brand.

I know this seems completely counterintuitive to many companies. They often ignore complaints left online on blogs, Twitter, Facebook, and other social sites. Yet, it's been proven for years that when companies directly engage with their detractors, the level of negative sentiment in these conversations decreases. In 2006, when it decided to start directly engaging with its online customers, Dell Computer determined that 49 percent of all conversations concerning its brand were negative. At first, Dell addressed only technical issues and complaints, but eventually it began responding to brand mentions as well, when appropriate. In less than two years, Dell saw the percentage of negative comments online about the brand fall from 49 percent to *just 22 percent* in 2008. By joining the conversations that customers were having about Dell, Dell was changing those conversations. And the change was obviously for the better.

This improvement also underscores a very important point: most customers that leave negative feedback about your brand online *want* your brand to respond! Typically, these customers aren't simply trying to attack your brand (although that does happen on rare occasions). Instead, they are usually trying to get your brand's attention because they want help with their problem! This explains why Dell and many other brands have seen a sharp decrease in the volume of negative online conversations concerning their brands when they started engaging with these customers directly and trying to help them. If these customers were simply trying to attack the brands, then the volume of negative conversations wouldn't have changed. Instead, they simply wanted the brand to help them with their problem, and when the brand did so, negative conversations decreased and positive conversations increased.

So now that we've established that responding to customers directly can help convert them from detractors into fans of your brands, what's the process for correctly engaging with angry customers online? First, make yourself aware of any specific laws that may govern your particular industry when it comes to directly engaging with customers online via social media and other channels. Some industries have strict guidelines governing what you can and cannot say to customers, and some forbid direct contact at all. So do your homework; talk with your company's legal department and see if there are any special considerations that apply to your particular industry.

When you encounter a negative comment or criticism online about your brand, there's a very important rule you should remember: every online conversation has three sides. There's your side, my side, and the side of *everyone else who is watching our interaction.* That last side is key, because *how* you respond is often as important as *what* you say online. For example, if your tone in responding to a customer is hateful and snippy, that is likely to anger other readers, and they may be tempted to send a hateful and snippy message back to you. On the other hand, if your tone is friendly and respectful, then that encourages other commenters to respond in kind. Always remember that *how* you respond to a criticism online is far more important than the criticism itself.

So how should you respond to a negative comment, tweet, or post left online? There are seven things to remember.

1. Respond as quickly as possible.

Take as long as is necessary to craft a proper response, but not a second longer! Remember that once a customer has left a complaint about your company online, the longer it sits there without a response from you, the greater the chance that additional negative comments will be left. If you take two hours to respond to a negative comment, you may have to address only that one comment, whereas if you wait two days, you might have to address five additional negative comments left after the first one. And when you do respond, clearly identify your role with the company.

2. Listen to and empathize with the commenter.

Read everything that the commenter has said, and also the content that he is responding to. For example, if the commenter is responding to a blog post about your brand, read that blog post and all the other comments to the post. If the commenter is responding to someone on Twitter, go back and find all the tweets in the exchange. The point is, you don't want to jump to conclusions about what motivated the person's comment. Try to find and read all the content associated with the comment so that you will have a better idea of why the person said what he did.

3. Be thankful that the person left the comment.

Always thank the person who left the comment. Even if it is negative, she is doing you a favor by bringing a problem to light. And it's better that she tells you what the problem is so that you have a chance to correct it than that she says nothing and switches to a competing brand!

4. Be respectful of the person who left the comment.

You may think that the person is dead wrong, but you need to understand that he might think that *you* are dead wrong. If you lower your guard and actually respect his opinion and listen to it, you may find that he will do the same. And remember, everyone else is watching how you engage with this customer. If you are respectful toward your customers, others will pick up on that. If you aren't showing your customers the proper respect, others will pick up on that as well.

5. If the customer has posted inaccurate information or if her comment is based on inaccurate information, feel free to correct her.

This often happens, and again, another way to minimize it is to respond quickly, before assumptions based on inaccurate information can spread. One of the case studies I'll cover later in this chapter will deal with a company handling negative comments based on inaccurate information.

6. Tell the customer how you are going to address the complaint and what the next steps are.

This communicates to the customer that you are taking his complaint seriously, and that you have a plan in place to handle the issues. Remember, most negative comments online are left because the customer wants help with his problem. If you can communicate to him that the problem will be taken care of and how that will happen, that will usually satisfy him and help convert him from a ranter into a raver.

7. Give customers a way to stay in touch with you, and invite further feedback.

Again, you have to consider that many customers are watching the interactions that you are having with other customers. By giving the customer a way to stay in touch with you, you communicate to that customer, and to everyone who is following your exchange, that your brand is serious about solving this customer's issue. This reflects well on your brand and can give even those people watching your exchange with the customer a more positive opinion of your brand.

Bonus Tip

Respond to your customers via the same channels and with the same tools. In December 2011, right before Christmas, a FedEx customer posted a video of a driver delivering his new computer monitor (video: http://www.youtube.com/watch?v=PKUDTPbDhnA). The "delivery" consisted of the FedEx driver parking his truck at the curbside, grabbing the computer monitor, walking up to the customer's gate, and literally tossing the monitor over. What's worse, the customer was at home when the driver arrived, and the front door was wide open. All the driver would have had to do was ring the bell at the gate. Instead, the monitor was damaged, and the customer posted the video of the delivery on YouTube. Not surprisingly, the video went viral, and garnered millions of views.

The video of the FedEx driver tossing the customer's computer monitor over his gate was uploaded to YouTube on December 19, 2011. This created a nightmare crisis management scenario for FedEx for two reasons. First, the video was posted right before Christmas, when many customers were buying and shipping last-minute Christmas gifts. For these customers, this video didn't make a strong case for choosing FedEx rather than a competitor like UPS to deliver those Christmas gifts. But second, the video was posted just six days before Christmas. No doubt a lot of key executives had already begun their Christmas vacations, making it even more difficult for FedEx to quickly pull together an appropriate response to the growing customer backlash.

Yet that's exactly what FedEx did. Just 48 hours after the customer's video was posted on YouTube, FedEx posted its own video response from Matthew Thornton, senior vice president of FedEx Express Operations for the United States (video: http://www.youtube.com/watch?&NR=1&v=4ESU_PcqI38). In this video, Mr. Thornton did three key things:

1. He admitted the problem and apologized for it immediately.
2. He detailed what had been done to correct the problem.
3. He detailed what would happen moving forward.

The video was also posted on FedEx's blog, along with a transcript (http://blog.fedex.designcdt.com/absolutely-positively-unacceptable). The post is the most commented on post on FedEx's blog by an almost 3:1 margin. But what's really interesting to me is the nature of the comments. More than half (57 percent) of the comments on the post are positive, and only 18 percent are negative! Many of FedEx's customers defended the brand in their comments and applauded Mr. Thornton's response. Granted, there were some complaints and a few "this happens all the time" statements, but

BACKSTAGE PASS!

IN THIS CHAPTER, we are dealing with customers who are upset with your brand, or who have a question or complaint about it. These are customers who typically are not fans of your brand, but if you handle their issues properly, you just might convert them.

We've already discussed seven things to remember when you are interacting with customers online, but when you are dealing with detractors (or ranters), here's what you need to do.

First, identify who is leaving the negative or critical blog post, tweet, or Facebook update about your brand. For our purposes, we'll consider four possibilities, and here's how you deal with each of them. (Keep in mind the seven steps for responding to online criticism that we covered earlier in this chapter.)

1. An unhappy customer.

If you encounter online criticism from an existing customer, you need to know who within your brand should respond to her. Should it be someone from your customer service team, or should it be a subject matter expert (SME)? Based on your brand's resources, you should identify anyone who is qualified to deal with customers online, then create a work flow so that you know which person or team should be notified about a customer complaint, based on the content and context of that complaint.

2. Someone who has inaccurate facts concerning your brand.

If someone is posting inaccurate information about your brand or your company, you want to respond to that and correct the information as soon as possible. For example, if a journalist or

continued...

blogger posts that your company doesn't provide healthcare for its employees (when it does), then you want to correct that information because it could result in criticism of your company. Always feel free to correct misinformation about your brand, but remember to do so in a polite manner and with a respectful tone. And make sure you check the facts with the appropriate sources internally so that you have *your* facts straight before you offer to correct someone else.

3. A content creator, blogger, or member of the media.

In recent years, there has been an explosion in long-form content devoted to product reviews being created on blogs and websites. So you might eventually encounter a blogger, for example, who reviews one of your products and offers a critical review of it. These bloggers are typically creating their content as a service for their readers, so you should consider working with them. Contact them, invite them to let you know if they want to review any of your brand's products in the future, and tell them that your brand will be happy to give them any additional information that they might need. Or if you feel that the blogger's review was based on inaccurate or incomplete information, politely offer to correct that information or provide additional information that you think might help the blogger. If you are respectful in your tone, most bloggers will pick up on that and actually appreciate your attempts to help them.

4. People who are out to pick a fight.

Rarely, you may encounter a person who seems to be going out of his way to attack your brand. He may be using abusive language or making claims that are obviously untrue. Often, these people are making abrasive comments simply because they are trying to provoke a response from others—especially the brand.

If someone leaves an abusive comment on your brand's blog, you are within your rights to delete that comment. When I say abusive, I mean using language that attacks a particular person (either someone at the brand or another customer or reader) or that is purposely disruptive. If someone leaves a comment saying that your brand sucks, it's probably not a good idea to delete that comment. Then again, if that person leaves that same comment every day and you warn him to stop, but he continues, then yes, you should probably delete the comment and possibly block the person from commenting on your blog. Usually, people who are trying to be disruptive and start a fight online are pretty easy to spot. Others spot them as well, and they won't fault your brand for deleting their comments on your blog.

Now tying into this point, you may have heard social media experts recommend that you *never*, under *any* circumstances, delete a comment that's been left on your brand's blog. It's true that you should try not to delete comments that have been left on your blog, but sometimes it's necessary. In general, however, it's always better to err on the side of letting the comment stand, unless it contains content that you feel is personally abusive to your brand, its employees, or other commenters. Just remember that if your brand starts deleting comments from readers, it exposes you to a higher level of scrutiny from those same readers, so it's best to have your ducks in a row before you start zapping comments.

Remember to always follow the seven rules for interacting with customers online and have a game plan for deciding who within your brand should be made aware of each complaint you find online, based on the type of person making the complaint (unhappy customer, someone with inaccurate facts, member of the media, or someone trying to start a fight).

there were more than three times as many positive comments as there were negative ones. FedEx changed the conversation about its brand by participating in that conversation.

It's vital that you not only create a response process, but also educate those of your employees who will be in contact with online customers on how to execute that process. Your employees need to understand what their roles are and the chain of command when they encounter negative feedback that needs to be addressed.

Let's look at two examples of companies that handled negative online feedback from their customers correctly and two that did not.

How Hardwood Artisans Overcame a Misunderstanding about Health Insurance for Its Workers

In 2009 I received a tweet from my friend Alison Burtt, who at the time was the director of marketing for Hardwood Artisans. Earlier that day, Hardwood Artisans had received a wonderfully positive article reviewing the business and its owner in the *Washington Post* (http://voices.washingtonpost.com/washbizblog/2009/01/value_added_12.html). Normally, this type of free publicity is cause for celebration, but Alison was quite upset. Several readers had misinterpreted the article and thought the writer was saying that Hardwood Artisans did not offer health insurance to its workers. When Alison alerted me to the article, it already had six comments, and all of them were negative.

Yikes! As you can see, Alison had plenty of reason to be upset about the reaction to this article when she contacted me and asked me how she should respond. I gave her the same advice I mentioned previously, and she crafted an absolutely perfect response to these negative comments. She did the following in her comment:

1. She immediately identified her role with Hardwood Artisans.
2. She thanked the readers for their feedback.
3. She politely corrected the misconception that her company doesn't provide health insurance, and was even smart enough not to put the blame on the writer in the process.
4. She shared her e-mail address with readers and invited follow-up.
5. She was completely respectful of everyone involved.

After Alison left this comment, the entire tone of the comments changed. A total of 16 comments were left on this post after hers, including 4 more from Alison. Of the 12 comments left by readers after Alison left her first comment, *none* were negative.

Additionally, something very interesting happened: Hardwood Artisans' fans started commenting and defending the brand! Several of them detailed how they had been buying from Hardwood Artisans for years and would continue to do so, praising the high quality of its products.

Isn't that a thing of beauty? By joining this discussion and responding appropriately, Alison completely reversed the flow of the conversation. Not only did the detractors disappear, but Alison's response galvanized Hardwood Artisans' fans to comment! Alison later told me that she received several e-mails from Hardwood Artisans customers and even complete strangers thanking her for responding to this article, and telling her that they appreciated her being involved.

How the Red Cross Avoided a Social Media Crisis and Inspired Its Fans

In the previous example, Alison acted smartly in responding to negative comments left about her employer on another blog. But what if one of your employees does something online that reflects negatively on your brand? How does your brand handle this correctly in order to avoid the dreaded social media backlash?

On February 15, 2011, Gloria Huang tweeted to one of her friends that she had gotten the beer and they were going to drink it later that night. Now, there's nothing wrong with this, until you factor in that Gloria accidentally tweeted this from her employer's Twitter account. And her employer happened to be the Red Cross.

Yikes! Gloria was using a tool called HootSuite to manage her tweets, and it seems that she simply forgot that she was still signed into the Red Cross Twitter account when she left that tweet. It's quite an easy mistake to make, but it still gave her employer a bit of a black eye.

To the Red Cross's credit, it reacted quickly to Gloria's tweet, deleting it within the hour. In addition, Gloria went to her personal Twitter account, explained the situation, and clarified that she had meant to send the "rogue tweet" from her account instead of that of the Red Cross. This could have been a very bad situation for the Red Cross, but it averted much of the negative reaction to this episode by responding quickly and telling everyone exactly what had happened. By acting quickly and transparently, the Red Cross not only defused the situation, but gave its fans a reason to rally to its defense. In fact, many fans started using the infamous #gettngslizzerd hashtag as a way to increase blood donations to the Red Cross! The Red Cross's fans decided to take ownership of the situation and turn a potential negative into a positive for the organization.

One way to create fans of your brand is by speaking in a human voice. The Red Cross did this; it quickly admitted its error and apologized. It also did so with humility and a splash of humor. Then Gloria tweeted an explanation as well. How the Red Cross handled this potential crisis situation went a long way in rallying its fans and advocates to come to its aid. They quickly forgave Gloria for the tweet, then took the hashtag and used it to drive donations.

Both Hardwood Artisans and the Red Cross turned what could have been a very negative situation for their brands into a very positive experience. What would have happened if either brand had not responded? Each situation would have only gotten worse, and with the Red Cross example, since the comment had been made on Twitter, if the organization hadn't responded quickly and appropriately, this situation could have become very negative for it very quickly. The Red Cross social media team deserves a big pat on the back for how it handled this situation.

Remember these examples if your company ever finds itself in a potential social media crisis situation. It's not the initial event that causes the potential crisis; it's how the brand *responds* to that event. Both Hardwood Artisans and the Red Cross responded appropriately to a potentially negative situation involving the brand, and each turned it into a positive situation. The brands in the next two examples weren't as successful.

Groupon's Super Bowl Ads Miss the Mark, as Does Its CEO's Nonapology

During the 2011 Super Bowl, Groupon ran a series of commercials that confused and angered many viewers. Each commercial featured a celebrity such as Elizabeth Hurley or Timothy Robbins. For the first few seconds the celebrity talked about an issue, such as the Brazilian rain forests are facing deforestation or that "The people of Tibet are in trouble. Their very culture is in jeopardy." Then the commercials immediately switched gears and related how Groupon users could get a great deal on a Brazilian wax or could get $30 worth of Tibetan food for only $15 by participating in Groupon deals. The intended humorous tone of the commercials missed the mark for many viewers, who felt that the commercials were mocking very serious world issues, and perhaps could even be seen as being exploitative toward certain people. Mainstream media outlets such as ABC

News (http://abcnews.go.com/Business/groupon-super-bowl-com mercial-ignites-controversy/story?id=12856998#.T9OBFNVYvu8) and the *New York Times* (http://dealbook.nytimes.com/2011/02/06/ groupons-super-bowl-debut-raises-ire/) wrote about the negative reaction that viewers had to the spots, which only brought more awareness of the commercials.

To his credit, Groupon CEO Andrew Mason addressed the backlash to the commercials on the Groupon blog (http://www. groupon.com/blog/cities/our-super-bowl-ads-and-how-were-help ing-these-causes/) the next day. When responding to negative feedback, responding as quickly as possible is the first step. Andrew published the post on the blog explaining Groupon's rationale behind the commercials within 24 hours.

Unfortunately, the tone of Andrew's response didn't endear either him or Groupon to many of the upset viewers. If your brand ever faces a backlash from your customers, especially online, remember that you do *not* have to apologize if you feel you have not done anything wrong. However, it's always a good idea to communicate to anyone that you have offended that you do sympathize with her feelings, and it's probably a good idea at least to apologize for causing those feelings.

Groupon CEO Andrew Mason did not apologize for creating and running the Super Bowl commercials that offended so many people. To be fair, if he truly believed that those commercials were true to his company's culture, he shouldn't have apologized for them. However, Andrew also didn't apologize for the fact that many people were upset by the commercials. He easily could have added the following clarification to his blog post: "We felt the commercials were consistent with our culture, and would ultimately bring awareness and aid to the causes mentioned within the spots. However, we also realize that some viewers may have misinterpreted our intent, and may have been upset by these commercials. To these viewers, we apologize." A response such as this would have communicated to everyone that while Groupon was standing behind its decision to create and run the commercials, it also had empathy for any viewers who were offended by them.

Many of the post's readers mentioned Mason's tone in their comments. Admittedly, there were many comments from readers saying that they loved the ads, but there were far more from readers saying that they found the ads offensive. Many stated that they wouldn't do business with Groupon again.

When dealing with a social media backlash from your customers, a company's most powerful weapon is two words from its CEO: we're sorry. Groupon didn't say those words, and that, coupled with Mason's tone, probably made the criticism of the company a bit louder. Remember, even if you feel that your company wasn't wrong, it always pays to have empathy for your customers' feelings and to understand their point of view.

Nestlé Unintentionally Fans the Flames on Facebook with Its Responses to Customers

In March 2010, probably for the first time, we saw a major brand face a crisis situation on its Facebook page. Greenpeace has long put pressure on companies that the organization feels are harming the environment in the creation of their products. In early 2010, Greenpeace went after Nestlé on several fronts, including its Facebook page, over its use of palm oil in some of its products, such as Kit Kat. The organization contended that acquiring palm oil not only leads to deforestation, but also threatens some animal species, including the orangutan. Greenpeace encouraged activists to post comments on Nestlé's Facebook page speaking out against the use of palm oil in the brand's products, and many of them also changed their profile picture to one of several altered Nestlé brand logos that ridiculed the brand.

Nestlé quickly posted to its Facebook page notifying everyone that if a comment was posted by someone using an altered version of Nestlé's logo, the comment would be deleted. Nestlé has every right to want to protect its branding. But when you tell anyone online that you will delete his comments, even if you are in the right, it's like waving a red flag in front of a bull.

Unfortunately, the company's responses on Facebook became increasingly incendiary and even condescending. Nestlé's tone on its Facebook page not only didn't help to stop the angry comments from users, but probably made the situation far worse. Granted, the brand was clearly unprepared for such an organized attack by Greenpeace and its supporters, but it did itself no favors by not only arguing with commenters on its Facebook page, but also mocking them. This simply led to more and angrier comments that Nestlé had to deal with. It also led to coverage in the mainstream media over how Nestlé was handling those comments on its Facebook page (http://news.cnet.com/8301-13577_3-20000805-36.html).

Finally, cooler heads prevailed and Nestlé admitted its mistakes and apologized on its Facebook page.

How You Handle the First Conversation Leads to the Second One

How to handle negative feedback online is one area of online marketing and social media management that is seriously misunderstood by many brands. Note that in all four of the case studies in this chapter, the eventual outcome was determined by how the brand responded. Hardwood Artisans and the Red Cross responded quickly and appropriately, and turned a potential crisis situation into a positive for the brand. On the other hand, Groupon and Nestlé both responded insensitively to the criticism the brands were receiving, which only intensified the backlash.

In all four instances, the first conversation involving the brand was negative. Hardwood Artisans and the Red Cross followed the steps outlined earlier in this chapter, and spoke in a human and compassionate tone. As a result, the conversation concerning each brand changed and became more positive. These case studies were chosen to make the point that *your brand has the power to change a conversation by participating in it.* In fact, if your brand responds correctly, negative comments about your brand can be your best chance not only to cultivate new fans but to galvanize existing ones.

The lesson: Your brand has the power to control the outcome of a potentially negative situation by how you respond. If you fail to respond, then you are ceding power to your brand's detractors. You are hoping that they will lose interest and move on. The cold reality is, these conversations won't go away. Your customers have more tools than ever before to create content and share opinions.

In 2012, Pew Internet found that 46 percent of U.S. adults owned a smartphone. That percentage was up from 35 percent the previous year (http://pewinternet.org/Reports/2012/Smartphone-Update-2012.aspx). This means that roughly half the adults in the United States have with them at all times a tool that lets them create videos, take pictures, and send tweets and posts immediately to Twitter, Facebook, their blog, and many other social sites. But you don't have to look at the studies; you can see this as you go about your day. Notice how many people are walking around holding a smartphone. They are holding a very powerful content creation tool—one that lets them create content about your brand.

Does knowing that excite you or scare the hell out of you? Either way, it's the new business reality. Your customers can create content about your brand and self-organize faster than you can. Hopefully, you'll see this not as a problem, but as the enormous opportunity that it is, and embrace it as such. Never before have fans of your brand had more ways to create content about you, and never before have you had more tools and channels to connect directly with them, and they with you.

The tools and technology may change, but this fundamental truth of business has not: those brands that adapt to change and embrace it, thrive. Those that do not, perish.

PART 3

BUILDING A
FAN-CENTRIC COMPANY

CHAPTER 7

How to Organize Your Employees So They Can Better Connect with Your Customers

I've been building the case for understanding and connecting with your biggest fans by showing you how rock stars connect with their fans and reap the rewards of having a close relationship with their most passionate customers. I've provided examples of brands that apply some of the same techniques that rock stars use to better connect with their own fans and customers. Along the way, we talked about how you can apply these same lessons to your own marketing and communication efforts in order to cultivate advocates for your brand.

Now it's time to take everything we've learned so far, and apply it to building the foundation for creating a truly fan-centric brand. In the remainder of this book, I will walk you through exactly what will need to happen to put your brand in a position where it can truly be connected to its biggest fans, and they to it. I've been fleshing out the ideas for *Think Like a Rock Star* since 2007, but in 2011, I started interviewing marketers working at some of the largest brands on the planet. My intention was to learn more about their efforts to better connect with their brand advocates. After talking to marketers for a dozen or so major brands, I came away with two takeaways.

1. Not a single brand I talked to had a formal process in place that connected it to its fans, and vice versa.

At best, a few brands were monitoring what their customers were saying about the brand online, and would reach out to those customers that supported the brand's efforts. But not a single brand had a brand ambassador program or any official process in place that allowed it to connect with its most passionate customers. To be honest, I was very surprised to learn this.

2. Every brand I spoke to said it wanted to become better connected to its fans, but didn't know how to get started.

These brands realized the importance of connecting with their most passionate customers, but they weren't moving forward with doing so because there wasn't a formal process in place to make those connections happen.

Based in large part on those conversations, I decided to create a formal process for brands that want to better connect with their fans. Over the course of the final five chapters, we'll look at what needs to happen at your brand, both internally and externally, in order to create a truly fan-centric brand. Along the way, we'll also look at examples from brands that are currently implementing and utilizing the processes that we're discussing. We're going to build on the methodology that rock stars use and apply that process to your brand.

First, the 30,000-Foot View of Becoming a Fan-Centric Brand

Before we get started on the specifics, let's back up and get a basic understanding of how rock stars build such powerful connections with their fans. There are several points to keep in mind when you think about the process of cultivating fans of your brand.

1. Participating in a conversation changes that conversation.

Right now, your customers are having a conversation that is related to your brand. When your brand begins to participate, the tone and makeup of that conversation will begin to change. And if your brand can participate in that conversation in a way that adds value to the conversation for your customers, this can be a very powerful tool in your efforts to cultivate advocates for your brand. We talked about this concept extensively in the previous chapter.

2. Interaction breaks down walls.

Almost every brand has two distinct types of conversations happening around and about it. There are the internal conversations that the brand has about itself, and there are the external conversations that the brand's customers are having about it. Usually, these two types of conversations are somewhat or completely different, because the brand and its customers aren't interacting. But when the brand and its customers start to engage with each other, the viewpoints and directions of the two distinct conversation types begin to become more aligned. Recall that in the first chapter we talked about how rock stars are fans themselves. This means that they are closely connected with their fans and, as a result, they understand the conversation their fans are having, and their fans understand the conversation the rock star is having. As a result, the two conversations are more closely aligned.

3. Interaction leads to understanding, and understanding leads to trust.

The more interaction you have with your customers, the easier it is for you to understand their viewpoints as well as their wants and needs. Likewise, if your customers have more interaction with your brand, they are far more likely to understand your point of view.

Rock stars have always understood this, which is a big reason why they seek out engagement and interaction with their fans. They understand that not only will doing this lead to a better understanding of their fans (and how to create the music and products that those fans want), but it will also lead to their fans trusting them and promoting the rock stars to their friends and other fans.

4. Trust leads to advocacy.

This is another key point that rock stars have always understood. If your customers don't trust you, they won't advocate on your behalf. And they can't trust you if they don't understand you. And they can't understand you if they don't interact with you and understand your point of view. So rock stars cultivate fans by interacting with them, embracing them, and engaging them. Those interactions lead to understanding, which leads to trust, which leads to advocacy.

With this process in mind, it seems obvious that the road to becoming a fan-centric brand starts with the brand's gaining a better understanding of its customers and connecting with them more often, and its customers with the brand. With this in mind, here's what our first rough draft of the process for becoming a fan-centric brand looks like.

1. We need to design a process that increases communication from the brand to its customers and from the customers to the brand.

Are there ways in which we can encourage feedback from our customers via our existing marketing and communication efforts? For example, do we give our customers a way to leave feedback on our blog and website?

2. We need to encourage both the brand and its customers to send and receive feedback based on their interactions.

This flow of feedback needs to move in both directions. Once we receive feedback from our customers, we need to communicate with them. This tells our customers that their feedback will be taken seriously, which will encourage them to leave even more feedback for the brand.

3. We need to take the internal (brand) and external (customer) feedback and derive relevant insights from it.

This is a vital step in the process of becoming a fan-centric brand. When we begin to collect valuable insights from the feedback we receive, we can act on those insights in order to see true benefits to our business.

4. The insights gathered from the brand and customer feedback need to be distributed to the appropriate people, both internally and externally, who can act on those insights.

There's no point in gleaning the proper insights from customer and fan feedback if we can't then distribute those insights to the people within our brand who are best poised to act on them.

5. There needs to be a mechanism in place, both internally and externally, that facilitates the flow of interactions and feedback both to and from internal (brand) and external (customer) sources.

We want to see communication from the brand to the customer and from the customer to the brand, but we also want to find a way to increase the level of interaction. More interactions lead to a higher probability that the brand and the customer will understand each other. This results in a higher probability that your customers will trust your brand, which increases the likelihood that they will advocate on your behalf. So we want to place a premium on a system that not only creates interactions between the brand and the customer, but also facilitates the flow of information and feedback both to and from the brand.

The process for becoming a fan-centric brand hinges on better connecting with our customers, getting feedback both to and from them, and then acting on it. Let's start laying the groundwork for becoming a fan-centric company by first addressing the need to better understand and connect with our customers.

From the brand side, we need to consider the conversations that our customers are already creating and participating in online. Specifically, we need to focus on three areas.

1. Monitoring.

Your brand needs to actively monitor what your current and potential customers are saying, not only about your brand, but also about your competitors and even your industry. Not only does this help your brand better understand your customers, but it can also help you deal with potential crisis situations and provide more effective customer service.

2. Drawing relevant insights from customer conversations.

Your brand can't act on your customers' conversations until you decide *what* is worth acting on.

3. Distributing insights to the areas within your brand that can best act on them.

This is where the rubber meets the road. Once you've decided what should be acted on, getting that information to the right people is imperative.

In a perfect world, your brand would already have a social media marketing team in place that is handling all three of these communication areas for your brand. But remember that we are interested not only in what our customers are saying, but in what our fans are saying as well. Also, we are monitoring the conversations our customers are having because we want to help convert these customers into *fans of our brand.* So for each of the three areas, we need a slightly different approach if our end goal is to cultivate more fans of the brand. Let's look at each area now with a view toward becoming a more fan-centric company.

Monitor Customer Conversations

Ideally, your company is already monitoring online conversations about and around your brand and your industry. In recent years, most brands have begun creating and hiring social media teams, and one of the core responsibilities of these teams is to monitor online conversations. But if your brand is not monitoring what your customers are saying online, let's first talk about how to get a team and a system in place to make that happen.

First, the size of your team will obviously be greatly affected by your budget and your resources. Many brands that have a mature monitoring program have two main staffing components:

1. A centralized team or "hub" that analyzes trends in customer conversations and data, and also helps to facilitate real-time interactions with customers, as necessary.

2. Decentralized teams or "spokes" that work on information and data sent from the hub, as well as acting on information that each spoke comes in contact with. These could be organized around different brands and product lines or around different tools—say, a team for Facebook and one for Twitter.

In general, think of the hub as focusing more on trends and the big picture, and the spokes as focusing more on real-time interactions. Now, what happens if your brand doesn't have the resources to staff both a centralized team and individual spokes? Which area should take priority? My advice would be to focus on training every employee who comes in contact with customers (especially online) in how to use social media effectively. By doing this, you are ensuring that when your employees encounter a situation online— for example, a customer is asking a question about a particular product—they can step in and help that customer as soon as possible. In the last few years, many bigger brands have begun training their employees on how to interact with customers via social media tools. The extensive step-by-step instructions for responding to customers online in Chapter 6 is a perfect starting point for training your employees.

You haven't trained your employees in how to use social media and interact with your customers online? That's okay, because now you can begin crafting a training program that focuses not just on responding to your customers, but on doing so in a way that is more likely to convert them into fans. Remember that when we are discussing the idea of cultivating fans of your brand, we are adding a new layer to your monitoring efforts. For example, let's assume that your brand already has a social media team in place, and that the members of that team are actively monitoring customer conversations online. They are probably actively tracking customer sentiment, and hopefully they are looking for customer complaints so that they can address those complaints. But is your team responding to online feedback from your fans? Probably not.

Most brands are standoffish toward their fans. We need to work on changing that if we want to transform your brand into one that is truly fan-centric.

We need to recognize that when we are monitoring feedback from our customers and from current or potential fans, we are trying to accomplish two things. First, we are looking for opportunities to engage with our brand's fans and to begin the process of connecting with them. Think of it as trying to get on their radar. We want to reach out to them and begin the communication process.

But remember that our long-term goal is to have a much closer connection with our fans as a whole. And in order to truly accom-

BACKSTAGE PASS!

AS YOUR BRAND is monitoring your customers' online conversations, whether you are using tools as elaborate as Radian6 or as simple as Google Alerts, you want to think about tagging the content your customers are creating, so that you can review that content when appropriate. When we talk about tagging content, we mean putting a label on it so that you can better identify it internally. For example, if a blogger writes a post about a negative experience she had when she tried to place a phone order with your company, you might tag that blog post as "Customer Service—Phone" and send it to Jessica, who handles all content with that tag. The reason why tagging is important is that it helps your brand bring customer conversations to the attention of the people within your brand who are best poised to act on them. For example, all customer

continued...

mentions of a particular product line might be tagged so that the brand team for that product line sees them. All technical questions about a particular product line might be tagged so that a particular subject matter expert (SME) sees them and can respond.

There are three main ways you can tag customer conversations.

1. Tagging conversations based on content.

When you are tagging based on content, you are looking for brand or product mentions. It's more about *what* the customers are talking about. If a customer sends a tweet about buying a particular model of swing set for her child, that tweet might be tagged internally by that brand so that the product's brand manager can see it. Then the brand manager can decide whether or not he should engage with the customer.

2. Tagging conversations based on context.

When you are tagging based on context, you are looking more at *why* a customer said what she did. If the customer tweeted about buying a particular model of swing set for her child and complained about putting it together, then that could change how you want to tag that tweet internally. Does the tweet still go to the brand manager for that product line, or do you tag it as being a potential customer service issue and route it to the customer service department so that it can respond?

3. Tagging conversations based on the customer.

You also want to pay attention to who is talking about your brand or product line. Susan Beebe explained to me that Dell does this, paying close attention to which influencers are driving the conversation around the brand. "We will spot people that are influencers around a particular topic, and we may flag them, so we can respond to them or have a certain SME respond to them. For example, if someone has a question about a server or Linux or some offering or capability that Dell has, I may tag a particular SME and ask him to respond to that customer. So we're not just listening, but we're also trying to connect them to SMEs within Dell. You have a decentralized model where everyone is listening and engaging more and more around whatever their specialty is within Dell."

You can easily add a layer to the tagging process and also tag when your fans are discussing your brand or your product lines, or even your industry. And since you've already been putting together a list of your fans as you completed the Backstage Passes I've left for you in the previous chapters, you already know whom to be looking for.

Whatever your tagging strategy is, you need to make sure that your monitoring team (or any employee who monitors online conversations) knows what to tag and who should receive the information within your brand. If you see a person complaining about your brand's customer service, for example, you need to know whether that complaint should go to the brand manager or to the customer service department. Plus, you need to know which person should see it.

In general, it is usually easier to tag conversations based on content (such as brand or product mentions) if you have fewer resources for monitoring customer conversations. As your team expands, you can drill down and start to look at not just brand mentions, but the context of those brand mentions. Either way, start by thinking about the tagging strategy associated with your monitoring efforts. Start by determining who will see what when it comes to tagging, and which conversations they should be seeing.

plish that, we need to empower our fans themselves to help us make that happen. In the Backstage Passes, we talked about starting the process of identifying who your brand's fans are, so that you can start to connect with them. While you are doing this, you also want to see if you can identify your more proactive fans, or "superfans," who will help you connect with other fans and help them connect with your brand. These will be the fans who are probably already making efforts to connect with other fans of your brand, without your help. For example, as I mentioned earlier, I am a big fan of Dr. Pepper. But while I am a fan of the product itself, I have no desire to start a blog, a Facebook page, or a LinkedIn Group devoted to my love of Dr. Pepper. Yet what if I did? What if I created a site that not only talked about my love of Dr. Pepper, but also served as a sort of home base for other fans who loved the product? Dr. Pepper would no doubt want to connect with me, because I had created a community where the brand's fans were connecting with one another.

Think about this as you are monitoring your customers' conversations. You are looking for fans of your brand, but you are also looking for the more proactive fans, the hand-raisers who are actually working to connect your brand's fans with one another and with your brand. These special fans will also be prime candidates to be involved in any brand ambassador or customer advisory programs that you wish to launch. We'll talk about both of these areas in the next chapter. If you already have a social media training program in place for your brand, all you need to do is apply the lessons from this book and add a layer to your training that addresses cultivating fans of your brand.

Another very important reason for considering training for employees who will be connecting with customers online is that you want to ensure *consistency of brand voice*. This is especially important if multiple people are monitoring a brand presence, for example, if a team of three people is in charge of your brand's Facebook page. Dell does a great job of keeping a consistent voice online, and I asked Susan Beebe, who at the time was a member of Dell's Global Communications and PR team, to talk about how the company does this. Beebe explained:

> *The thing I tell people is, look at the brand's voice. Dell has always had a direct-to-customer model. It's the soul of Dell, coming from Michael Dell. So you take on the brand's personas and values, and you speak and operate in that way. A lot of people will ask me how we can have seven or eight people working on one Dell Twitter account and not sound different. The truth is that we are really good about understanding the voice of Dell and applying it to social media. It humanizes the brand, and it also makes it consistent and reliable. So customers are getting a consistent experience with Dell across all of our social profiles.*

As customers, we expect a consistent experience when we interact with brands online, don't we? Think about visiting your favorite chain retailer or restaurant. You know that no matter what branch of the chain you visit, you are going to get pretty much the same experience. Each store will have roughly the same layout, you'll get roughly the same level of customer service at each location, and so on. Brands work to create a consistent voice, and this needs to extend to your efforts online. It's another reason why training your employees works, as it has for Dell.

Draw Relevant Insights from Customer Conversations

Hopefully, your brand already has an employee structure in place that allows it to draw relevant insights from online customer conversations and data. If your brand is already mining customer conversations for relevant insights, we need to add a new layer here. We want to draw relevant insights from existing customer feedback and conversations, with the end goal being to *create more connection with your fans and to better understand them.*

In the Backstage Pass in this chapter, we talk about tagging conversations that you find your customers engaged in online so that you can act on them. This is the same idea; we want to monitor what your customers are saying online, and then draw insights from those conversations so that we can act on them. When you are attempting to draw insights from these conversations, here are a few areas to pay attention to.

1. What is the context of the conversations that your fans and your customers are having concerning your brand?

What are they praising, and what are they complaining about? What areas of your brand are driving the conversation? This will also help you determine the identity of your brand's fans. Understanding the reasons why your fans love your brand is crucial to creating and building a deeper relationship with them.

2. What attributes of your brand are driving conversations, and are those conversations positive or negative?

When you are monitoring customer conversations, you want to look at several different areas. For example, you might look at the conversations that are happening that involve the product itself: its design, how it functions, and so on. You could also look at what customers are saying about your customer service, and maybe even break it down to their feedback on the customer service they receive in your brand's retail locations versus online. The point: when you start measuring and studying the conversation level and tone concerning different brand attributes, it becomes easier to notice differences. And these differences are usually a clue that will help you identify how your customers and fans truly perceive your brand. It also helps your brand identify both potential problems and potential opportunities.

3. What are the opportunities?

As you monitor your brand's space, are you seeing conversations concerning areas that your brand isn't addressing? Are the new features on a competitor's smartphone creating a buzz among customers? Is another competitor's new web-based customer service delivery model getting high marks from online customers? Remember that what's working for the competition could work for you as well. Likewise, if the competition does something that upsets its customers, it's a good idea to learn from that, and not make the same mistake at your brand.

Distribute Insights to the Areas Within Your Brand That Can Best Act on Them

Now that you've been monitoring the conversations that your fans and customers are having online and have begun drawing insights from the data, we want to make sure that those insights make it to the people within your brand who are in the best position to *act* on them.

For example, let's say that you track the sentiment of the online conversations involving the customer service your brand provides, both online and in a retail setting. The conversations concerning customer service are 77 percent positive for your retail locations but are only 41 percent positive when customers are purchasing from your brand's website. Customers cite several problems with your online customer service, such as slow load times and no real way to ask questions or get more information. So from your monitoring, you know that faster load times and a live-chat mechanism with customer service agents on the website would result in higher customer satisfaction with the online buying process.

But the question remains: *Who* should receive these insights? Should they go to the brand manager? The online customer service manager? The IT department? All of the above? You need to create a work-flow system so that you understand how to route information and insights within your brand. In this example, it looks as if adding live-chat functionality to the website would be a smart move, but there may be a real reason why this isn't possible. So instead of alerting the IT department that it needs to add live chat to the website, it probably makes more sense to alert the brand manager and have her decide whether adding live chat to the website is feasible or not.

To simplify the process, especially if your brand doesn't have a robust monitoring structure in place, it might be a good idea to think about creating "buckets" for your insights, then distilling from there. For example, you might send any generic brand insights to the brand manager and any generic customer service insights to the customer service department. In the previous example concerning adding live chat to the website, that insight could be flagged as a customer service issue and go to the customer service department. The customer service department could analyze the insight, then work with the brand manager to decide whether adding live chat to that brand's website would be a good idea or not.

The idea is to have a structure in place so that everyone who is monitoring and analyzing your customers' online conversations knows where any relevant data or insights should go within your brand and your organization. Obviously, each brand will have a different internal infrastructure, but the key is to put the system in place to route the information.

CHAPTER 8

How to Organize and Mobilize Your Customer and Brand Advocates

In the previous chapter, we discussed a monitoring system and ways of drawing insights from what your fans and customers are saying online, then distributing those insights internally so that they get to the people within your brand who can best act on them.

My goal is to help your brand do a better job of cultivating fans. One of the main reasons rock stars have fans is that they strive to have a close connection with their fans. If we want the same thing for your brand, we need to create a way for your brand to have more direct contact with your fans, and vice versa. We need to think about how we can organize your fans, both *internally* and *externally*.

Internal Collaboration Tools for Your Employees

As social media tools for individuals have become more popular, companies have begun to roll out similar solutions for companies.

The result is that there are now a myriad of collaboration tools available to your brand that allow your employees to work together quickly and easily to not only better understand your fans, but interact with them as well. These tools can be anything from simply giving your employees chat functionality to giving your brand its own social networking site. Here are a few examples of how this could really benefit your employees.

1. Collaborate on handling customer service issues.

Let's say a member of your customer service team is on Facebook and finds a complaint from a customer. The employee could take that Facebook update and send it to your brand's social networking site, where every employee who is a member of the site can see it. Then, as a group, your employees can work together to find the proper response to this customer.

2. Ask each other questions.

Maybe you have a question about how to properly respond to a customer, or maybe you simply have a tool-specific question that you need an answer to as soon as possible. Having a platform available for your employees would be a great way to allow them to immediately tell who is online and available for them to help each other.

3. Share and collaborate on ideas.

You might have heard of Dell's IdeaStorm site. It's a wonderful platform that allows Dell customers to submit ideas, and other customers can vote them up or down. It's a great way for Dell to find out what product features, for example, its customers want, and the brand often implements the more popular customer submissions. But Dell also has an internal version of IdeaStorm just for its employees. This is a great way for employees to bat ideas off one another; in the process, everyone learns together.

4. It gives your employees a backup.

If one of your employees encounters a customer issue that needs immediate attention, it's great to know that he has a tool available that will let him connect with other employees quickly to discuss the situation. And putting another set of eyes (or three or four sets) on a situation never hurts!

5. If your company has a lot of virtual employees, a collaboration tool is a must.

If all your employees are in the same building, then an online collaboration platform is very convenient, but if half your employees are in another time zone, it's a necessity.

6. Online collaboration tools can improve employee morale and build connections.

MarketingProfs is a virtual company. According to its chief content officer, Ann Handley, it is constantly making use of online collaboration tools such as Skype for chatting, Basecamp for project management and managing day-to-day work flow, and Dropbox for storing and moving video and audio files as well as other assets. MarketingProfs also has a private Facebook group just for its employees. I asked Ann why she felt that was important for the company.

> As a virtual company, there are lots of tools we can use for productivity. But true camaraderie is trickier. So we use a Facebook private group as a kind of water cooler/break room to foster personal connections between all of us (that's where we celebrate birthdays or new babies or new puppies

*or whatever!) as well as to call out folks internally for a
job well done or other recognition. Sometimes, folks talk
about weekend plans, what they made for dinner, or what
their kids are up to. The platform gives us a community
feel without actually being in the same physical location. It
doesn't replace face-to-face connections (that's important,
too), but it can augment it.*

Another consideration is that using these tools to build community and morale is a great way to encourage your employees to use the other online collaboration tools that you offer. If your employees start participating in your private Facebook group, it increases the likelihood that they will start connecting with other employees via the Chatter or Yammer social network that your company has set up.

No matter which tools you use, it's a good idea for your employees to have ways to connect with one another quickly and easily.

Core Functionalities for Your Team

I don't want to spend too much time covering individual vendors and tools because collaboration tools for the enterprise are evolving so quickly that much of the vendor-specific information I could give you as I am writing this book is likely to be outdated by the time you read it. Instead, let's talk about the core functionalities these tools can provide for your team.

1. Instant messaging/chat.

This is similar to what you've been using for years. It's a quick way for employees to connect with one another and discuss an issue in real time.

2. Wiki or editable online documents.

This functionality is useful when a team is collaborating on creating a central document for the brand—for example, if your brand wants to create a set of guidelines for how you should interact with your fans. The core document could be created, then team members would have the ability to go in individually and change certain parts of the document, or mark certain areas so that the rest of the team members can add their comments.

3. A social networking site.

This could be very similar in look and functionality to the popular social networking sites you are used to, such as Facebook. The advantage here is that this site can be an all-in-one tool for your brand, a tool that lets you chat with other employees, work together on documents as a wiki would, and share information with other employees and build camaraderie the way MarketingProfs does.

4. E-mail.

Good old-fashioned e-mail is still a great way to collaborate with your employees. Don't forget that many of your employees may actually prefer e-mail to other forms of communication.

Build a Brand Ambassador Program for Your Fans

Now that we've talked about finding ways to connect the employees who will be connecting with your fans, let's move our attention to creating a way to bring your fans together. Let's talk about building a brand ambassador program.

First, what *is* a brand ambassador program? A brand ambassador program brings together special customers who not only are fans of your brand, but also take passionate ownership of it and want to work with you to promote it to other customers. These are fans who will start conversations with other customers and will go out of their way to expose them to your brand. Although promoting your brand to other customers isn't the only expectation, it's typically the chief goal of brand ambassador programs. The idea is to find fans of your brand who are passionate and outgoing and are already actively promoting your brand to others, and give them better tools for doing so.

Let's look at a couple of examples of brand ambassador programs.

1. YouTube's marketing ambassadors program.

YouTube launched this program in early 2012. It picked nine businesses from across the United States that were successfully using YouTube as a marketing tool to grow the business. Since these businesses were selected based on how well they were leveraging YouTube as a marketing tool, their participation in this program was dependent upon their sharing what they have learned. For example, upon joining the program, each business immediately picks a nonprofit organization and begins mentoring it on how to use YouTube effectively to build awareness for its organization. In addition, the nine businesses that are part of this program will periodically participate in Google Plus hangouts and contribute marketing materials and advice for other businesses.

YouTube structured this program by first finding businesses that were performing well using YouTube as a marketing channel, then having members teach others what they had learned. Not only does YouTube benefit because the program helps bring more businesses to the site, but other businesses benefit as well because they are receiving mentoring and advice from a business that has had proven marketing success on YouTube. It's a win-win proposition.

2. Maker's Mark's brand ambassador program.

Maker's Mark has one of the most successful and longest-running brand ambassador programs. Maker's Mark was a small distillery in Kentucky that made one thing very well: bourbon. The company had a very passionate but very small customer base and wasn't well known outside the state of Kentucky.

But all that changed in 1980 when the *Wall Street Journal* published a front-page article on the company, its distillery, and its founder. Overnight, there was national interest in the small Kentucky distillery, and the company received more than 25,000 letters as a result of that one *Wall Street Journal* article (http://www.dcgourmet.net/archives/131). This created two big problems for Maker's Mark. First, its bourbon took six years to age, so the next batch was several years away. And that batch was only large enough to supply the local customers in Kentucky that loved the bourbon, not the entire country. Second, Maker's Mark didn't have a national distribution system in place. It could service Kentucky, but that one *Wall Street Journal* article had created a firestorm of national interest in the brand, and Maker's Mark didn't have the supply or the distribution to meet that demand.

The first issue that Maker's Mark had to address was sustaining this sudden wave of interest in the brand for the next few years until there was more of Maker's Mark available for sale. Many people from all across the country who had read about Maker's Mark in that *Wall Street Journal* article were now looking for its bourbon, and they couldn't find it. So Maker's Mark started reaching out directly to its customers, not only in an effort to keep a dialogue going with them, but also to help them locate whatever supply of Maker's Mark bourbon was actually available in stores across the country! Also, Maker's Mark asked its customers to request their local stores or restaurants to carry Maker's Mark bourbon. This increased interest among customers was a signal to distributors that they needed to order more Maker's Mark.

At this point, it's important to talk about Maker's Mark's founder, Bill Samuels. Samuels hated marketing and felt that it was quite rude to promote your product openly. He believed that friends don't market to friends, and since he viewed his customers as his friends, he didn't want to market to them. In general, Samuels didn't want to "get in the face" of his customers; he wanted his customers to discover his brand, and then he and they could develop a relationship. He felt that it wasn't right to promote a product to customers who hadn't shown an interest in it, but if a customer was interested in Maker's Mark, then the brand could develop a relationship with that customer.

So Maker's Mark had always put a premium on having a personal relationship with its customers, and specifically with those customers who had shown an interest in supporting the brand. In other words, Maker's Mark wanted to connect with its most passionate fans. And in the early years, when most of the customer base was located in Kentucky, the company knew a good percentage of its customers personally. But as the company's growth accelerated through the 1980s and into the 1990s, that growth created a sense of distance between the company and its customers. Long gone were the days when the founder knew many of his customers as personal friends; the customer base had expanded from Kentucky across the entire country.

The question became, how could Maker's Mark continue to have a close relationship with its customers now that it was a national brand? In 2000, the company found its answer. It launched a brand ambassador program that allowed it to work with its most passionate fans across the country. These fans would not only attempt to convince others to try Maker's Mark, but also talk to stores and bars and encourage them to carry its products. Ambassadors are treated as though they "work" for Maker's Mark and it is their "job"

BACKSTAGE PASS!

LET'S ALSO TALK about how big your brand ambassador program should be.

Obviously, the size of your program will be to some extent determined by your available resources. Having more members means having more people to manage and work with. So if your brand is launching an ambassador program for the first time, it's better to start small. There's a very practical reason as well: this is a learning opportunity for your brand. When you are launching any type of program for the first time, you *will* make mistakes, so it's better to make those mistakes (and learn from them) on a smaller scale.

So what's the right size for your program? If you are launching a brand ambassador program for the first time, I would suggest starting with no more than 10 brand ambassadors. I would review that number in a year's time and see if you want to keep it the same, reduce it, or expand the size of the program. Also, if in a year's time you decide to expand the enrollment in the program, you can reach out to your *existing* ambassadors to help you find new candidates.

Finally, working with a smaller program means that it'll be easier to track and measure how effective the program is in helping your brand grow. It's far easier to start with 5 brand ambassadors and expand to 25 than it is to start with 25 and realize that you can handle only 5!

to promote the brand to others. Among the perks for members of the ambassador program is their own barrel of whiskey, which is fermented for six years (which extends the fan's "ownership" of the brand and makes it literal). Her name goes on the barrel, and when it is ready to be sold, she gets the first chance to buy a bottle from it. Additionally, she can visit the distillery at any time and see her barrel.

A brand ambassador program made sense for Maker's Mark because as the brand grew, its managers became concerned that they were losing the ability to talk directly with their customers. Through this program, Maker's Mark has a direct connection with the brand ambassadors, who *then* have a direct connection with other customers. The point is that this program became a reality because it was born out of a desire by Maker's Mark to have a constant, direct connection to its customers. The main motivation for the program was to maintain that close connection with the customer, because that was an essential part of the Maker's Mark brand.

A brand ambassador program works for Maker's Mark because wanting to pursue a close relationship with its customers and to treat them as if they were close friends is in the brand's DNA. Launching a brand ambassador program means that you are committing not only to giving some of your most passionate customers greater ownership of the direction of your brand, but also to having that close relationship with them. You should welcome the chance to do both these things if you want to see an ambassador program succeed for your brand.

Lay the Groundwork for a Brand Ambassador Program

Here are 10 steps to creating a successful brand ambassador program. As you are reading, you'll see how many of them connect back to the earlier work we've covered in this book, especially in the Backstage Passes found in each chapter.

1. Realize from the beginning that creating a brand ambassador program means losing control.

The very heart of a brand ambassador program is the concept of empowering the ambassadors to spread the message about your brand, in *their* space. Think of this as a shift from your brand sending marketing signals to the customers, to giving the customers the ability to market to each other. If your company is not willing to relinquish the control necessary to begin a brand ambassador program, then the process needs to end here. Additionally, your brand needs to understand that as your brand ambassador program matures, your ambassadors will naturally assume a greater level of ownership and that your brand will have *less* say in its structure and function. This may seem scary at first, but you will eventually realize that it's a good thing.

2. Decide why you want to start a brand ambassador program and what your relationship with its members will be.

Just as with any other marketing effort, you need to start out by deciding what it is you want to accomplish. What do you want your relationship with your ambassadors to be? In the YouTube example, its marketing ambassadors are asked to play the role of teacher. YouTube wants its ambassadors to share what they know because that will show other businesses the marketing potential of YouTube and encourage them to start using the site as well. Maker's Mark wants its ambassadors to encourage restaurants and bars to carry the bourbon and to thank those that do. Its ambassadors communicate that there is a demand for Maker's Mark, which will result in more sales.

3. Decide whom you want to join your brand ambassador program.

After you've decided what you want to accomplish with your brand ambassador program, it's easier to decide which fans will make the best brand ambassadors for your program. Maker's Mark wants ambassadors who not only have an appreciation for its whiskey, but also are outgoing and don't mind striking up a conversation with another customer or a bartender and encouraging him to try or carry Maker's Mark. The role you want your ambassadors to play will help you decide on the ideal candidates for your program. *Hint:* This is part of the reason why I wanted you to start identifying who your fans are in earlier chapters, especially the Backstage Passes. If you've been doing this, you now have a head start on identifying who could be right to join your brand ambassador program!

4. Make membership a privilege.

You don't want to open your brand ambassador program to all your fans. You want to open it only to the special customers who are committed to doing the work required to grow the program—and your brand. As I mentioned earlier in the book, I love Dr. Pepper. But I would not be a good candidate for a brand ambassador program for Dr. Pepper, because while I love the product, I'm not committed to going out and talking to other customers and trying to convince them to drink Dr. Pepper. You want your brand ambassadors to view it as their *responsibility* to help grow your brand. You want them to be the fans who truly feel ownership in your brand, and that's why you need a screening process. You need to conduct interviews. Watch your fans and how they interact with other customers online and, if possible, offline as well.

5. Quality trumps quantity.

Would you rather have a brand ambassador program with 10 highly engaged members or one with 1,000 members who signed up only to get a free T-shirt? You want your brand ambassadors to be highly engaged and *passionate* fans. You want them to have the type of passion for your brand that's infectious and that rubs off not only on other ambassadors, but on your brand as well! Don't focus on the size of your program; even if you start with only five superpassionate fans, that's fine, because those fans will attract others who love your brand as much as they do.

6. Connect with your advocates and create ways for them to connect with one another.

Your fans are special. You don't want them on an island; you want them connected. In the Maker's Mark example, I mentioned how ambassadors get their names put on a barrel of whiskey as it ages for six years. There are 30 ambassadors who "own" each barrel, and Maker's Mark sets up an online forum so that these "barrelmates" can connect with one another and form a bond.

7. Pay your ambassadors.

This is one of the biggest misconceptions about brand ambassadors. They *do* want to be compensated, but most of them do *not* want to be given money. They want access. Think about fans at a rock concert. What do they want? They want a backstage pass! They want to go behind the curtain and see the "secret" stuff that's happening. In Chapter 1, Katie Morse from *Billboard* talked about how musicians are using social media to let their fans see what's happening in their lives "behind the scenes." Your fans are the same way; they want special access. They want to see your new line of products three months before the products go on sale. When I worked with Dell on its #DellCAP event, one of the highlights for Dell's fans was getting to spend 30 minutes talking to CEO Michael Dell. This is a level of access that most customers will never have, and it helps identify these fans as special. In addition, it gives them greater access to the brand, which helps deepen their ties to it. So if you want to think about how to pay your ambassadors, think about how you can give them an experience that your regular customers can't have.

8. Make sure your ambassadors have direct access to your brand.

This is a necessity for the development of the program, but your ambassadors will also view it as a perk and another advantage of being involved with the program. Additionally, you want your ambassadors to always have a way to contact your brand so that they can share what they are seeing and hearing from other customers out in the field. Also, make your ambassadors responsible for reporting directly to the C-suite; give them the task of providing progress reports, recommendations for improvement, and the like to your brand. Remember, as much as possible, you want to treat them as if they are employees performing a job. Give them ownership, because that's what they want.

9. Transfer ownership of the program from the brand to its ambassadors.

As mentioned in the first step, when you create a brand ambassador program, you need to realize that in the long term, this program will belong to your fans. You'll always be there, and you'll always have a voice, but the idea is that eventually, you want your most passionate customers to take over this program. At some point, your current brand ambassadors will help you select the proper candidates to join the program. At first, your brand may work closely with the ambassadors to manage the program, but as time goes by, you want to gradually shift more ownership of the program's direction to its members. Ultimately, your fans are going to have more passion for this program than your brand ever could, and that's why you need to empower your fans to take the reins, because they are the ones who will be connecting with other customers and representing your brand.

10. Create a leadership council for your brand ambassador program.

This is a small group that will oversee the program itself and its direction. A good size is four or five members, with two or three of them being customers who are current members of the brand ambassador program. At least one member will also be the chairperson of your brand advisory panel, as detailed in the next chapter. You want to ensure that your customers make up at least half the members of this group, or the majority if you have an odd number of members.

What Comes Next?

In the previous chapter, we talked about ways to better organize the information and conversations that your customers and fans are creating. We also talked about how to break down the information and insights gained from those conversations based on content as well as context. In this chapter, we built on that and talked about mechanisms that your brand can use to better organize internally and externally, including how to facilitate collaboration among your employees and how to organize your fans through an external brand ambassador program.

Now we're ready to take the next step and talk about how to create teams on both the brand and customer sides that will help ensure that the voices of your fans are heard within your brand, and vice versa.

CHAPTER 9

How to Empower Your Fans and Employees

We want to design a process that not only helps you to analyze information from your brand's fans, but also facilitates feedback and communication between your brand and its fans. To help us achieve this, we need to create two teams: an internal team that works primarily with your brand's employees and an external team that works primarily with your brand's fans and customers. Each group has the task not only of helping to communicate feedback from one group to the other, but of acting on that feedback when appropriate.

These two groups are the brand advisory panel (BAP) and the customer advisory panel (CAP).

1. Brand advisory panel (BAP)

This is an *internal* group based within the brand. Its main responsibilities include:

★ Ensuring that the customer advisory panel receives all relevant and appropriate information from the brand. Essentially, the BAP wants to ensure that the CAP hears and understands the brand's point of view.

★ Ensuring that the BAP receives feedback from the CAP as well as providing feedback to the CAP.
★ Overseeing the brand ambassador program.
★ Meeting quarterly with the brand's key executives to give them greater insights into and understanding of the brand's efforts to connect with and understand its customers and fans.
★ Working within the brand to ensure that relevant customer feedback and insights are distributed to the areas of the brand that can best act on that information.
★ Working within the brand to help create a structure and framework to encourage collaboration among employees who deal directly with customers.
★ Providing employees with education on how to connect with customers and cultivate fans of the brand.

Ideally, the BAP has four members, of whom three are employees and the other is a customer or fan of the brand. This last member should also be a member of the CAP.

2. Customer advisory panel (CAP)

This is an *external* group located outside the brand that represents your customers. Its main responsibilities include:

★ Ensuring that the brand hears and understands the voice of the customer.
★ Ensuring that the CAP receives feedback from the BAP as well as providing feedback to the BAP.
★ Providing the BAP with relevant information from the customers, including complaints, suggestions for improvement, areas of praise, and so on.
★ Acting on feedback from the BAP by communicating with customers on an ongoing basis.

The functions, responsibilities, and staff descriptions for both the BAP and the CAP are meant to serve as guidelines and as a starting point for your brand. This is not a one-size-fits-all model, so don't get hung up on trying to follow the structure given in this chapter to the letter; instead, focus on what you are trying to accomplish. The end goal of both the BAP and the CAP is to improve the flow of information and connection between the brand and the customer, and vice versa. For example, maybe your brand can't afford to have three employees on your BAP. Perhaps you can manage only two employees and one customer. That can still work. It's far more important to find a solution that works for *your* brand than to try to follow these guidelines to the letter.

An easy way to understand the difference between the BAP and the CAP is to remember that the brand advisory panel is within the brand, while the customer advisory panel is the voice of your customers.

Staffing Breakdown of the Brand Advisory Panel

As mentioned earlier, the BAP should have four members, three from the brand and one customer. For most brands, it makes sense to have these employees also perform other roles within the brand. For example, the employee performing the role of brand liaison may also be an assistant brand manager. For larger brands, it may make sense to treat each of these positions as full-time.

Let's take a closer look at the various roles and their responsibilities.

1. BAP chairperson

The employee in this role has the following responsibilities:

★ Overseeing the BAP itself and making sure that everyone does his job and understands his responsibilities.

★ Assisting and working with the CAP to ensure that both groups are meeting their goals and objectives.

★ Working with the leadership council of your brand ambassador program to oversee and work with its members to facilitate growth and value creation for both its members and the brand. This was described in the previous chapter.

★ Developing and overseeing an employee education program for engaging with the brand's fans. Ideally, the brand is already providing an employee education program for social media; if so, this program could work in conjunction with that program.

One-third to one-half of the employee's time should be devoted to carrying out these responsibilities.

2. Fan insights and collaboration officer

The employee in this role has the following responsibilities:

★ Ensuring that insights from the brand's fans are derived so that they can be communicated to the brand. This employee works with the CAP to ensure that those insights are delivered to the appropriate people within the brand so that they can act on them.

★ Working with the brand to ensure that it has and is using the proper collaboration tools so that employees can better organize and better connect with the brand's fans.

★ Working with the BAP chairperson to ensure that the employees of the brand understand how to use its collaboration tools.

★ Also serving as a member of the customer advisory panel.

Approximately one-third of the employee's time should be devoted to carrying out these responsibilities.

3. CAP liaison

This is a customer role with the following responsibilities:

★ Working with the CAP to ensure constant communication and a proper flow of information both from and to the CAP.
★ Also serving as a member of the customer advisory panel.

4. Brand liaison

The employee in this role has the following responsibilities:

★ Working with the CAP liaison to ensure constant communication between the BAP and the CAP.
★ Sending back to the brand information and suggestions on how the brand can improve its relationships with and understanding of its fans.
★ Working with the brand to send feedback from the brand back to the CAP.

Approximately one-fourth of the employee's time should be devoted to carrying out these responsibilities.

Staffing Breakdown of the Customer Advisory Panel

The customer advisory panel should have three members, two of whom are customers of your brand. Ideally, these two customers will also be members of your brand ambassador program, as discussed in the previous chapter. Preferably, they will also be members of the leadership council of your brand ambassador program.

Let's take a closer look at the various roles and their responsibilities.

1. CAP chairperson

This is a position for one of your customers. It has the following responsibilities:

★ Overseeing the CAP itself and making sure that everyone does her job and understands her responsibilities.
★ Assisting and working with the BAP to ensure that both groups are meeting their goals and objectives.

2. Customer communication officer

This is a position for one of your customers. It has the following responsibilities:

★ Overseeing the creation and execution of a framework for communicating directly with customers in order to relay information about the brand to them, and also collect feedback from customers that can be delivered to the brand.
★ Working with the fan insights and collaboration officer of the BAP to ensure that both units are meeting their objectives.
★ Taking the role of CAP liaison for the BAP.

3. Brand liaison

This is a position for one of your employees. It has the following responsibilities:

★ Working with the CAP liaison to ensure constant communication between the BAP and the CAP.
★ Working with the CAP to ensure that the voice of the brand is heard and understood in all activities.
★ Serving in the same role on the BAP, and above all working to ensure that constant communication between the BAP and the CAP is maintained.

Compensate Your Customers Who Serve on the BAP and the CAP

I encourage providing compensation for members of your brand ambassador program in the form of more access to your brand. However, for the customers who are involved in your BAP and CAP, because you are asking them for a specific and regular time commitment, it makes sense to treat them as part-time employees. As such, they should be compensated.

The amount of time required from your customers (especially those who are working with the CAP) won't be quite as much as you'll need from your employees, but you should still count on at least three to five hours a week per customer. Budget that amount for the first quarter, then see what your results are. If you're trying to secure a budget for this, any funds that your brand currently allots to focus groups, for example, could cover this instead.

I've Heard of Some Brands That Have a Customer Advisory Panel; Is This the Same Type of CAP That We Are Discussing?

In most cases, probably not. Some brands, such as Walmart and Disney, have programs that focus on connecting with social media influencers (some of whom may also be fans of the brand) in an effort to get product feedback and build awareness of the brand and its events. Such programs do have some of the elements that we've been discussing in this chapter, but they aren't quite the same thing.

A better example (on a larger scale than what your brand may need initially) is the Fiskateers program. Fiskars has a strict self-selection process to bring in fans of its brands. The company interacts regularly with the Fiskateers, and they actively work not only to promote the brand (through facilitating conversations involving scrapbooking), but also to engage with other customers. They are not just a promotional channel for Fiskars; they also serve as a *feedback* channel. This is an extremely important element that many influencer programs miss because those programs are focused more on connecting with influencers, who can then promote the

BACKSTAGE PASS!

INITIALLY, YOU MAY encounter internal resistance to the idea of investing a lot of time and effort in launching programs designed to help your brand better connect with its fans, such as the BAP and the CAP. This approach will probably be something that your brand hasn't attempted before, and there will always be pushback from some when you try something new, especially when it comes to marketing. In order to deal with current or potential resistance, you want to make sure that you highlight how making an effort to connect with your fans will benefit your brand. Here are a few ways in which connecting with your fans will have a positive impact on your brand.

1. More connections with your fans mean better data about your fans and customers.
This will be a big help to your brand's marketing efforts, since once your brand better understands your customers and fans, it can market to them more effectively. Your brand's marketing will become more efficient, which means that its marketing costs will go down. Also, if your brand is regularly investing in focus groups and other forms of market research, those costs can probably be eliminated by your proposed programs. In addition, the data you'll get about your customers will be far more accurate and meaningful.

2. As you engage more with your customers and fans, they can provide additional customer service resources for your brand.

This probably won't be an immediate benefit, but after your efforts to better connect with your fans have been in place for a while and are well established, you can work with your customers and fans to help them provide assistance and guidance to other customers. This will transfer some customer service functions away from your brand over to your customers, resulting in a cost savings for your brand. And it will mean fewer calls to your customer service center!

3. A closer connection with your fans means improved customer satisfaction and loyalty.

This will lead to an increase in positive sentiment online about your brand. Make sure your brand's social media manager understands this, because it will make the social media marketing team's job a lot easier. As your brand's fans become more active and vocal online, there will probably be less negative content and complaints from online customers. This means less work for your social media response team and customer service reps.

Remember that the best way to convince skeptical people within your brand that connecting with your fans is a good idea is to show them how doing so will benefit them directly. Show them how your proposed programs will make their jobs a bit easier. All of the previous points are examples of how connecting with your fans will help someone within your brand perform his job a bit more easily. We are still creatures who keep our own best interests in mind. If you can show me how your idea will make my work life a little bit easier, I will probably want to support your efforts!

brand to their networks. With our model of a customer advisory panel, not only do the members advise the brand, but the brand interacts with them as well. Then the customers interact with *other* customers and can give more thorough feedback to the brand.

Remember that your end goal in becoming a fan-centric brand is to put your brand in a place where you can better understand your customers and *they can better understand you.* We are designing teams such as the BAP and the CAP to facilitate interaction and communication, because that will lead to understanding, which will lead to both the brand and the customer advocating on the other's behalf.

Which Customers Should You Select for the CAP?

Many brands use a customer advisory panel, council, or board. However, because of the way many of these groups are designed, contact between the group and the brand is infrequent. Typically, there is an annual meeting and perhaps a conference call or two during the year.

We want your brand's customer advisory panel to be a dynamic group that is in constant contact with your brand and vice versa. One of the main goals of both the CAP and the BAP is to facilitate and improve the communication between the two groups, as well as between the brand and its fans. As to which customers would be the ideal candidates to join your CAP, here are a few of the characteristics to look for.

1. Customers who are passionate about your brand and love interacting with other current and potential customers.

Throughout this book, we've been laying out a framework for identifying the fans of your brand. Part of the reason for this is that you want to begin to understand who your fans are on an individual level. For example, you want to identify the fans of your brand who are proactively interacting with other customers, not just to promote your brand to those customers, but also to get their opinions and feedback about the brand. At this point, I need to make an important clarification: don't read this and think you simply need to target extroverted customers. One of the great things about social media, and I am saying this as an introvert, is that it gives introverts the ability to be more extroverted online. So don't think of what you are doing here as targeting extroverts rather than introverts or vice versa. Instead, you are looking for fans who are independently interacting with other customers on the brand's behalf.

2. Customers who have a business background working with similar brands.

This definitely isn't a requirement, but it can help. For example, if your brand operates in the tech sector, a customer who has experience working in that same space will not only understand your customers a bit better, but also understand your business and industry. Thus, she will have an understanding of both the customer and the brand. That could be of great benefit to your brand, especially if you use these customers as a sounding board to hear perspectives from both the customer and the brand.

3. Customers with good communication and listening skills.

Keep in mind that the members of your CAP will be encountering other customers both online *and* offline. Therefore, you want to pick customers who can actually engage with fellow customers, not people who can spout branding talking points. You want customers who can have a conversation with other customers and can follow up and figure out why a customer does or doesn't like your brand. The most important responsibility of your CAP is to ensure that the brand understands the voice of the customer.

4. Customers who understand that they are the brand's spokesperson "out in the wild."

You want the members of your CAP (and your brand ambassador program as well, for that matter) to understand how their interactions with other customers reflect on your brand. If they are courteous and helpful and make a sincere effort to listen to other customers, that reflects positively on your brand. If they become argumentative and defensive when other customers express a dislike of your brand, that obviously reflects poorly on your brand. You want customers who not only understand that they are representatives of your brand, but view this as an honor and always act in your brand's best interests.

CHAPTER 10

How to Help Your Brand Ambassadors Connect with Your Customers

Now that we've assembled your brand's internal and external teams, we need to get them working together to facilitate a constant flow of information and communication between your brand and your customers. Before we talk about what this structure and process should look like, let's back up for a moment and remind ourselves of the process that rock stars use to connect with their customers and cultivate fans.

Throughout *Think Like a Rock Star*, I've been giving you examples of how rock stars, past and present, have connected with their fans. Recall that in several of these examples, such as Taylor Swift holding T-Parties, Amanda Palmer's secret shows, or Johnny Cash performing at Folsom State Prison, there was a common approach. These rock stars created a way to connect with some of their most passionate fans in a *very* small group. They understood that connecting with their most passionate fans in a small and intimate setting strengthens the bond and affinity between them and their most passionate fans.

We've discussed why this is so important: because rock stars understand that their ability to attract new customers tomorrow is going to depend greatly on how well they understand and delight their fans *today*. Rock stars connect with their most passionate fans today, knowing that the efforts of these fans will result in the rock star's gaining new fans *tomorrow*. In contrast, most companies hope to gain new customers tomorrow by running a newspaper ad today. See the disconnect?

So how does this apply to your brand's efforts to connect with and understand your fans? Just as Taylor Swift rewards her biggest and most passionate fans with an invitation to her T-Party, you want your biggest and most passionate fans to be involved in your customer advisory panel and brand ambassador program for the same reasons. Your brand needs to understand that your ability to attract new customers tomorrow is going to depend greatly on your ability to understand and delight your fans *today*. In many respects, this entire process is about shifting control of your marketing and communication efforts to your fans. Why is this so important? Because when your marketing and communications efforts are done in the voice of your customers, they *resonate with your customers.*

Keep that in mind as you flesh out your brand's structure for connecting with your fans. You are looking to identify your biggest and most passionate fans and involve them in the process; then you want to empower them to constantly speak to other customers on your brand's behalf.

Create a Structure for Constant Communication Between Your Brand and Its Fans

Now we're ready to talk about how these various internal and external groups should work together in a real-world setting to help your brand better cultivate and connect with your fans. We'll be dealing with two internal groups (the brand advisory panel and the brand ambassador program) and one external group (the customer advisory panel).

1. Brand advisory panel

The brand advisory panel (BAP) will be in constant contact with both the customer advisory panel (CAP) and the brand ambassador program via its leadership council. Additionally, the BAP will report to the brand any relevant fan insights based on feedback received from both the CAP and the brand ambassador program. If there is a formal team or structure within your brand that handles such information, such as a customer insights team, then the BAP will relay those insights and information directly to this team. Otherwise, this information could be routed to your social media monitoring team, your customer service department, or perhaps your marketing team. Remember that the end goal is to make sure that the fan insights are put into the hands of the people within your brand who can best distill and act on those insights or route them to the group within your brand that can best utilize them.

2. Brand ambassador program

Your brand ambassador program will interact directly with the BAP and with its own members via its leadership council. In order to simplify the communications channels, the brand ambassador program will not interact directly with the CAP or the brand, but instead let the BAP communicate with both these groups on the program's benefit. This also helps to ensure that both the brand and the CAP are getting correct and consistent information from the brand ambassador program.

Help Your Customer Advisory Panel Connect with Your Customers and Fans

Now let's turn our attention to the customer advisory panel. The CAP will have indirect contact with the brand via the BAP, which it will interact with directly. But the CAP will provide a very critical additional function: it will advise the brand and the members of the brand ambassador program on how to interact with customers. Since we are building a process for your brand with an end goal of being able to better understand your customers as a result of an increased level of interaction with them, we need to set some ground rules for how your brand is expected to interact with your customers. Given its makeup, your CAP is in a perfect position to advise your brand on how to interact with its customers. Working with your CAP, you can craft guidelines for how your brand ambassadors can communicate and connect with customers. Here are some points to keep in mind.

1. They are *brand* ambassadors, not *product* ambassadors.

Your brand ambassadors should understand what it is about your brand that makes it unique. For example, if Apple used brand ambassadors, would they focus on the fact that Apple makes great computers, or would they focus on the fact that it is a brand that thinks differently, creating user-friendly products that do what you want them to do and are amazingly simple to use—some of which happen to be computers. Make sure your brand ambassadors understand what it is about your brand that makes it unique.

2. Your brand ambassadors are not marketers.

Never consider your brand ambassadors to be marketers. If you do, then they will believe that their job is to promote your products, and that's what they will do. Maker's Mark has a simple tenet for its brand, the idea that the brand will never invade a customer's airspace until that customer invites it in. Your brand ambassadors are there to interact with your customers and to learn from them and about them, but they are not there to promote your brand to people who don't want to hear your message. Doing so would reflect negatively on them, and on your brand as well.

How do you do this? For example, if you're a brand ambassador for Maker's Mark, you don't go to your favorite liquor store, stand by the whiskey section, and tell anyone who comes within sight that he should try Maker's Mark. But if, as you are leaving your favorite restaurant, the manager asks you about your experience, then she has given you the perfect chance to tell her that you thought the meal was excellent, but you were disappointed that the restaurant didn't offer Maker's Mark bourbon.

3. Constantly remind your brand ambassadors that listening is one of their core responsibilities.

The ability to get feedback directly from your customers is one of the key advantages of launching a brand ambassador program. At first this might not seem significant, but if you have 50 members of your brand ambassador program talking to customers all across the country, and the majority of them are hearing the same type of feedback about your brand, that's information that your brand might have never uncovered by itself. Constantly ask your ambassadors, "What are you hearing from our customers?"

Collect Feedback from Your Brand Ambassadors

One of the primary functions of your brand ambassadors is to collect feedback from your current and potential customers. As your brand ambassadors are interacting with customers in the

BACKSTAGE PASS!

ONE OF THE things you want to pay special attention to is giving your ambassadors a few guidelines to remember when they are interacting with other customers. These are not talking points; they are a few pieces of advice that your brand ambassadors should remember when they are "out in the wild." You should develop three to five points and make them simple and easy to remember. Here are a few examples.

1. Remember that you (the ambassador) want to listen so that we (the brand) can understand.
Yes, it's tempting to view your brand ambassador program as a way to increase sales, but remember that you don't want to turn the ambassadors into marketers. You want them to interact with other customers so that you (the brand) can get better feedback.

2. All feedback is important, even if it's negative.
Teach your ambassadors to prize negative feedback about your brand, because you can't correct the problems with your brand that customers perceive until you know what they are. Encourage your ambassadors to listen and understand when customers voice their displeasure with your brand.

3. Always remember that you (the ambassador) are the voice of the brand to other customers.
You must stress this point to your ambassadors. If they encounter a customer and treat him with respect and understanding, that reflects positively on your brand. However, if they get into

an argument with a customer, that leaves a negative impression of your brand.

4. Don't market to other customers, but do share your love of the brand.

Encourage your ambassadors to listen to other customers. If those customers mention your brand or if it makes sense to bring up your brand in a conversation, then your ambassadors should talk about it. However, your ambassadors shouldn't bring up your brand and its products unless the customer(s) they are interacting with show an interest. They should be there to provide information and insights, but not to force that information on customers who aren't interested.

Finally, a key bit of advice for you (the brand): *give your ambassadors a way to close the sale*. For example, if one of your brand ambassadors is discussing your golf clubs with another customer and that customer remarks, "Wow, I definitely need to check out those clubs," then what? You need to give your brand ambassadors a source of additional information that can move interested customers closer to a sale. It could be a website; it could be a customer service phone number. To help you quantify the ROI of your efforts, create a special URL or e-mail address or dedicate a phone number that your brand ambassadors can provide to interested customers. You can use your website's analytics to track how many times that special URL was accessed and see how many of those visits led to a sale. Again, we don't want you to view your brand ambassadors as solely being a way to generate sales, but by the same token we want to make sure they do have the information and materials they need to close a sale if they encounter a customer that wants to buy from your brand.

wild, you need a way to act on the feedback generated through those interactions so that you can derive actionable insights from them.

To accomplish this, you need to find a way for your brand ambassadors to record their individual interactions with customers, and also a way to summarize the information that your brand ambassadors as a group are receiving. In Chapter 8, we talked about collaboration tools that your employees can use to discuss the interactions they are having with your brand's customers. Consider creating a similar framework where your brand ambassadors can record their interactions with customers. This could be something as simple as e-mails sent to the head of the leadership council of the brand ambassador program, or maybe something a bit more elaborate like a social networking site or wiki created just for the brand ambassador program. One advantage of having brand ambassadors post their interactions online on a site or a wiki is that this allows members of the program to review and study what other members are seeing during their interactions with customers.

Once there is a structure in place that allows the brand ambassadors to share the results of their interactions with customers, the leadership council can then take the information learned from those interactions, summarize it, and offer suggestions and potential insights to the brand advisory panel (BAP), which can then share that feedback with the brand. Likewise, the consumer advisory panel (CAP) should also provide regular feedback and advice on interacting with customers and what the group is learning from doing so. The size of the brand ambassador program will play a big role in determining how often the BAP should provide customer feedback to the brand. For example, if the brand ambassador program has only five members, then quarterly updates may work best, but if the program has five hundred members, perhaps monthly or even weekly updates are the way to go. Likewise, the BAP should then relay feedback back to both the brand ambassador program and the CAP.

You've Created a Feedback Loop Between Your Brand and Its Customers

One of the biggest problems facing most brands today is that there are two completely distinct and disconnected types of conversations happening around and about them. You have the internal conversations that the brand is having about itself. These involve how the brand perceives itself, the market in which it operates, and its customers. Then you have the external conversations concerning the brand. These conversations are driven primarily by the brand's current and potential customers. Typically, most brands don't truly understand their customers, and the customers don't truly understand the brand. A big reason for this disconnect is that the brand and its customer have little or no direct interaction. The process outlined in *Think Like a Rock Star* has been designed to increase interactions between the brand and its customers. As the brand and its customers interact with each other, understanding begins to develop, and this results in the internal and external conversations becoming more aligned.

But How Do You Measure the ROI of Engaging with Your Fans?

Ah, the dreaded, "What's the ROI?" It's a question that has plagued social media and digital marketing professionals for years as skeptical marketers try to figure out whether all this social media stuff really works.

Since your efforts to cultivate fans will probably include a social media component, I think it would be a good idea to discuss how to determine whether your efforts are working. Let's use a very commonsense approach to determining the ROI of engaging with your fans.

First, when someone asks, "What's the ROI?" what she really means is, "How can we tell if this stuff is working?" I tell clients to ask themselves this question: "In order for this to be successful, what needs to happen?" Do the same thing with your efforts to engage your fans. For example, if you are going to launch a brand ambassador program, what needs to happen as a *result* of that brand ambassador program in order for it to be a success? What will success look like? How will you quantify it? Will it be a success if sales increase by 10 percent? If you see positive reviews on Amazon increase by 33 percent? Perhaps you want to see a 15 percent decrease in calls to your customer service center. Whatever your goal is, you need to start with a definite endpoint for your efforts. Once you define that ultimate goal, it will help shape all your efforts from that point forward. Let's say you decide that the goal of your brand ambassador program is to see a 33 percent increase in four- and five-star reviews of your product on Amazon over the next six months. Now that you have a set goal for your program, you can structure the program to meet that goal. You can encourage your ambassadors to write reviews on Amazon. You can also coach them on how to encourage other customers to do the same. When your ambassadors interact with a customer who's had a positive experience with your brand's product, they could encourage that customer to write a review on Amazon.

The point is, having a definite goal gives structure to all your efforts. Most brands struggle to determine the ROI of their social media marketing and fan engagement efforts simply because, instead of measuring the things that actually affect their goal, they measure the things that are easiest to track. This is why so many companies think that increasing the number of Twitter followers or Facebook Likes that they have is a viable return on their social media marketing efforts.

To measure the ROI of your efforts to cultivate fans of your brand, follow these steps.

1. Set a definite goal for your efforts.

In other words, write out what needs to happen in order for your efforts to be considered a success. If you are launching a brand ambassador program, say, "This brand ambassador program will be a success if in one year's time, _____ has happened." Whatever you put in that blank is how you will determine whether your brand ambassador program is working.

2. Structure your efforts so that they support your end goal.

If you want to increase sales, factor that into how you engage with your fans. If you want to get input from your fans on how to improve the design of your product, then focus on encouraging feedback from fans that will help you achieve that goal.

3. Use metrics that tie back to the ultimate goal of your efforts.

If the end goal is to increase sales, track either metrics that focus directly on increased sales or metrics that indicate the increased likelihood of a sale. For example, does gaining 23 followers on Twitter this week indicate an increase in sales? Probably not, so it's probably not a good idea to use it as an indicator of increased sales. But if you know that 10 percent of all visits to your product's landing page on your website end in a sale, then it makes sense to track traffic to that landing page. If traffic to your product landing page increases by 100 percent as a result of your brand ambassador program, and

10 percent of that traffic turns into a sale, then that's a real increase in sales as a result of your brand ambassador program. Measure what matters.

4. You can have multiple goals, but you should prioritize those goals.

Maybe you want to generate sales, but you also want to increase positive brand mentions online. Which goal is more important to your brand? You need to decide which goal is the priority, because that will help you structure your brand ambassador program, as well as your training for the members of that program.

5. Don't be afraid to adjust your goals.

You should review the progress of your efforts to connect with your fans on a regular basis. You should do this at least quarterly, but monthly or even biweekly is better. If you see or sense that a particular approach isn't working, feel free to tweak or change your methods. For example, if your brand ambassadors aren't doing a good job of encouraging the customers they interact with to visit your website, should they use a different approach? Or should they stop encouraging customers to visit your website at all? You need to study both your results and the tactics you are using to achieve those results. A lot of your efforts will be based on simple trial and error.

CHAPTER 11

What Comes Next

One night, as I was nearing the end of writing this book, I saw a blog post that Scott Monty had shared on Facebook. Scott is the head of social media for Ford, and he was sharing a post about a customer's experience with the brand. The customer had originally connected with Scott on Twitter and was a bit skeptical about Scott's enthusiasm for the brand and whether Ford was a company that really cared about its customers. He asked Scott a few questions; then a few months later, when the customer starting to consider a Ford as his next vehicle, he jokingly sent Scott a tweet asking him to tell Ford CEO Alan Mulally to contact him and convince him to buy a Ford. To the customer's surprise, Scott sent him a direct message on Twitter asking for his phone number, and sure enough, shortly thereafter, Mulally called this customer! He talked with the customer for about 30 minutes about his passion for the Ford brand, but he also wanted to learn more about the customer himself, who remarked in the post that Mulally seemed genuinely interested in his situation, which had included some negative experiences with a couple of Ford dealerships. After his conversation with Mulally, not only did the customer stay in touch with Ford at the corporate level, but multiple people from local Ford dealerships called him and, in the end, they worked out a deal to make his new vehicle purchase a Ford.

In 2010, Taylor Swift planned to do an autograph signing in Nashville as part of the CMA Music Festival. Now with most autograph signings, you end up standing in a long line for hours for the chance to spend $50 to $100 on an autograph from your favorite celebrity, whom you never meet because she stopped signing autographs after an hour even though there were 500 people still standing in line. Taylor's autograph signing was a bit different. First, she didn't charge any of her fans for her autograph. Second, she decided to make the autograph signing last a whopping *13 hours*, since 13 is her lucky number. Taylor started signing autographs for her fans at 8:00 A.M. At 9:00 P.M., when the signing was supposed to end, she could see that she still hadn't signed for everyone, so she extended the signing for another 2 hours. All told, Taylor spent almost 15 hours with her fans that day, performing for them and signing autographs for around 2,000 lucky fans. All for free.

Both of these stories clearly illustrate that the future of marketing belongs to the brands that strive to create *personal* connections and relationships with their customers and fans. Alan Mulally can't afford to spend 30 minutes on the phone with every potential Ford customer any more than Taylor can afford to spend 15 hours every day signing free autographs for her fans. But both Taylor and Ford can create a culture that makes every effort to prize personal communications and connections with customers more than impersonal advertising and marketing. Ford and Taylor can't scale having such personal communications with their customers and fans, but they don't have to. Their actions *create new fans who will spread that message for them.* I discovered the story of Alan Mulally's calling one customer because that customer blogged about it and Scott Monty shared it. If you do a Google search for "Taylor Swift 13-hour autograph signing," you will find dozens of articles and blog posts (even videos from the event) written before and after it occurred. People are drawn to the efforts of these brands and rock stars, and spread their messages as if they were their own.

A few years ago, when I started researching how rock stars connect with and cultivate fans, I suspected that there must be some secret formula that just makes it easier for rock stars to create fans. As we've learned from the myriad of case studies and examples so far in this book, most rock stars do two very simple things incredibly well. They relentlessly communicate two messages to their fans:

1. I appreciate you.
2. I love you.

That's it. There's really no secret formula, no secret sauce. Rock stars simply value and appreciate their fans.

The good news is, if you're reading this book, you probably already appreciate the importance of connecting with your brand's fans. The bad news is that there's no guarantee that the rest of the people involved with your brand will agree with you. You need to become an advocate for your brand's advocates. You need to make sure that your brand understands the importance and positive impact of connecting with its fans. You can use the case studies in this book to help you prove your point to skeptics. If your CMO doesn't understand why your brand should invest in creating stronger connections with your fans, show her the case study on the Fiskateers and how Fiskars's business has grown as a result. Show her the positive impact that Graco enjoyed after it embraced its core customers via blogging.

There are few true downsides to better connecting with and understanding your brand's fans. This may be a bit scary if your brand has never tried it, but it's a lot scarier to simply tread water along with your competition, isn't it? These social media and digital marketing tools are completely changing the relationship between brands and customers, and the smart brands are the ones like yours that are leveraging these changes for future growth.

This Book Isn't for Your Brand, It's for Your Fans

As we are winding down our time together, I have a confession to make. This book wasn't written primarily for you, my dear brand marketer. It was written *for your fans*. Yes, everything in this book will help you better connect with and understand your brand's customers, and if you use the guidelines in this book to cultivate better relationships with your customers and turn them into fans, this will have a *significant* positive impact on your brand's bottom line.

But as I was writing this book, my first consideration was always, *is this going to benefit your brand's fans?* Is this book written from the point of view of the people who love their favorite brands? Is it written in their voice? If your brand's fans could talk to you, does this book accurately reflect what they would tell you about who they are and why they love your brand?

I took this approach because ultimately, if you are acting in the best interest of your fans, you will also be *acting in the best interest of your brand.* This is a very powerful lesson when it comes to social media and really all forms of marketing: focus on making things happen indirectly. You want to provide a *direct* benefit to your target audience, because if you do this, your brand will *indirectly* benefit. Remember how Kaitlyn Wilkins let me ask Ford's CMO a question during an auto show? Kaitlyn understood that if she created a direct benefit for me, the marketing blogger (a chance to ask Ford's CMO a question), it would indirectly benefit her client by resulting in additional coverage for Ford on my marketing blog.

I've done the same thing with *Think Like a Rock Star.* I've written a book that will directly benefit your brand's fans. This book shows you how to better connect with and understand your biggest fans. This is exactly what your fans want: to be *more closely connected to and better understood by your brand.* This book directly benefits your biggest fans, with the understanding that it will *indirectly* benefit your brand.

This is all about blurring the line between brands and fans. We accomplish this by making sure that your brand *speaks in the voice of your fans*. I began this book by talking about how most advertising and marketing is wasteful because it doesn't create a connection with its intended audience. A big reason for this is that most marketing and advertising is done in the voice of the brand. It doesn't resonate with us because we don't understand the tone and voice of the brand, and because the brand doesn't understand us.

With *Think Like a Rock Star*, you now have the knowledge that will let you better connect with your fans and, more important, understand them. You can now let the voice of your fans permeate your brand and its communications. And your fans will listen and respond to your marketing because it will have been created in a voice that they recognize—their own.

Because your *fans* are the real rock stars. Your job is to build them a stage, give them a microphone, and listen to the beautiful music that they create.

Appendix

PREFACE

---

http://www-935.ibm.com/services/us/cmo/
   cmostudy2011/cmo-registration.html
2011 IBM survey conducted with over 1,700 CMOs to
determine their top marketing priorities for the next few
years.

INTRODUCTION

---

http://www.jeweljk.com/forum/index.php?topic=1093.0
The amazing story behind JewelStock.

http://www.kickstarter.com/projects/amandapalmer/
  amanda-palmer-the-new-record-art-book-and-tour
KickStarter page for Amanda Palmer's wildly successful
project, which raised over $1 million for the rock star.

CHAPTER 1

http://www.google.com/blogsearch
Google's Blog Search, which allows you to search blogs.

http://boardreader.com/
Board Reader, a search engine for message boards and
forums.

ttp://www.youtube.com/watch?v=1L3eeC2IJZs
The hilarious (and sometimes profane, so it's NSFW)
commercial Alamo Drafthouse created from an angry
voice mail a customer left after she was removed from
the theater for using her cell phone.

http://blogs.indiewire.com/thompsononhollywood/
  alamo_drafthouses_kicked_out_customer_worst_
  moviegoer_ever#
An article that references the praise that CNN journalist
Anderson Cooper heaped on Alamo Drafthouse's CEO
for booting the texter out of his theater.

http://www.youtube.com/watch?v=7ibFOA6c5Zk
YouTube video that shows the "grand opening" of a cake used in the promotion of *The Dark Knight*.

CHAPTER 2

http://thedonnasmedia.com/
TheDonnasMedia.com, an amazing site that has thousands of audio and video files of performances by the Donnas, all captured and submitted by the band's fans.

http://www.brainsonfire.com/work/view/fiskateers/
More information on the results the Fiskars brand enjoyed from launching the Fiskateers movement.

http://forums.pb.com/
Pitney Bowes' User Forum, where users help solve issues for each other, resulting in significant customer service savings for the brand.

CHAPTER 3

http://facebook-studio.com/news/item/page-publishing
   -that-drives-engagement
An interesting Facebook study of its most successful brand pages to see what type of content drove engagement.

http://www.homegoods.com/blog/category/all/
HomeGoods's wonderful Open House blog.

http://socialbutterflyguy.com/2012/02/22/video-king-
arthur-flour-uses-facebook-to-build-friendships/
A video interview that social media expert DJ Waldow
conducted with King Arthur Flour's PJ Hamel about
how the brand uses social media to connect with its
customers.

http://www.thecleanestline.com
Patagonia's blog, the Cleanest Line, a wonderful example of creating content that focuses on the bigger idea.

http://blogs.cdc.gov/publichealthmatters/2011/05/
preparedness-101-zombie-apocalypse/
The CDC's hilarious—and extremely successful—post on
raising awareness of the need to create an emergency
kit in order to survive the coming Zombie Apocalypse!

https://twitter.com/#!/CDCemergency
The CDC's Twitter account that gained *over one mil-
lion new followers* as a result of its post on the Zombie
Apocalypse going viral.

http://www.youtube.com/user/redbull
Red Bull's YouTube channel. Red Bull is actively posting
new videos to its channel, which is a big reason why it
has so many subscribers (the fact that the videos are
great doesn't hurt either!).

https://www.facebook.com/redbull
Red Bull's Facebook page, one of the most popular on
the Internet.

CHAPTER 4

http://www.youtube.com/watch?feature=player_
    embedded&v=eabtzkY_jNs#!
Blink 182's mashup of fan-created videos set to its song
"Up All Night."

CHAPTER 5

http://www.starbucksmelody.com/
The blog for Starbucks Melody, one of the best examples
of a fan-run blog.

CHAPTER 6

http://www.youtube.com/watch?v=PKUDTPbDhnA
Video that captured a FedEx driver carelessly tossing a
computer monitor over a customer's gate!

http://www.youtube.com/watch?&NR=1&v=4ESU_
    Pcql38
Video response from FedEx after one of its drivers was
caught mishandling a customer package.

http://blog.fedex.designcdt.com/absolutely-positively
   -unacceptable

Fed-Ex's post detailing its video response to a video that
showed one of its drivers carelessly handling a customer's computer monitor.

http://voices.washingtonpost.com/washbizblog/
   2009/01/value_added_12.html

Washington Post article that featured Hardwood Artisans. Pay close attention to the negative tone of the
first few comments; then notice how the entire conversation changed after a representative from Hardwood
Artisans joined the discussion.

http://abcnews.go.com/Business/groupon-super
   -bowl-commercial-ignites-controversy/
   story?id=12856998#.T9OBFNVYvu8

ABC News article documenting the reaction to Groupon's Super Bowl commercials.

http://dealbook.nytimes.com/2011/02/06/groupons
   -super-bowl-debut-raises-ire/

New York Times article detailing some of the negative
reaction and controversy surrounding Groupon's Super
Bowl commercials.

http://www.groupon.com/blog/cities/our-super-bowl
   -ads-and-how-were-helping-these-causes/

Groupon's CEO responds on the brand's blog to the reaction over its Super Bowl ads.

http://news.cnet.com/8301-13577_3-20000805-36
.html

CNET's coverage of the backlash that Nestlé faced on its
Facebook page over its policing of user comments.

http://pewinternet.org/Reports/2012/Smartphone
-Update-2012.aspx

2012 Pew Internet report on the prevalence of smartphone usage.

CHAPTER 8

http://www.dcgourmet.net/archives/131

Article detailing Maker's Mark's success after it was
featured in the *Wall Street Journal*.

Acknowledgments

I've been working on *Think Like a Rock Star* for about four years. During that time, I've been lucky enough to have had dozens of people help and support me on this journey. I could not be more thrilled with what this book has become, and I owe a debt of gratitude to so many people. I want to single out some of them here.

First, thank you to my mother, Carole, and my sister, Beth, for supporting me throughout this process. This book marks the end of one road, and I am incredibly grateful to you both for helping me during my first days on this path, when I wasn't entirely sure where it would lead.

Thank you to Lisa Petrilli for being a constant friend and giving me excellent advice on the direction of the book. And thank you for introducing me to my literary agent, Linda Langton. Linda, thank you for believing in the idea of this book as deeply as you did, and for your advice and mentorship throughout the publishing process. Thank you to my editor, Casey Ebro. Casey, you immediately got why the idea behind *Think Like a Rock Star* was so powerful. It was wonderful to work with someone who believed in the idea as much as I did. Your advice and no-BS style was just what I needed.

Additionally, many people went out of their way to help me with either the writing or the marketing of this book. Some agreed to let me interview them, some gave me marketing advice, and some gave me feedback on the book itself. Thank you, all, in no particular order: Amy Africa, John Moore, Greg Cordell, Lou Imbriano, Ekaterina Walter, Katie Morse, Melody Overton, Jackie Huba, Susan Beebe, Tom Martin, Ann Handley, DJ Waldow, Scott Monty, John Pope, Richard Binhammer, Kelly Hungerford, and Dave Gardner.

One thing that was amazingly cool about writing *Think Like a Rock Star* was that as soon as I announced the book, friends started asking me what they could do to support it. I am truly blessed to have friends who helped me get the word out on this book via their networks months before it would be on the shelves. Thank you to Drew McLellan, Beth Harte, Amy Canada, Victor Canada, Jenny-Rebecca Schmitt, Margie Analise, Susie Parker, Michael Rubin, Amy Fitch, and Jennifer Kent.

Thank you to all my friends at #Blogchat. I am incredibly humbled by the amazing community of helpful and supportive people that you have become. Many of the strategies in *Think Like a Rock Star* were either learned or validated by participating in the #Blogchat community and watching it grow. You are all very special people, and I am grateful to know each and every one of you.

Finally, a special thank you to Kathy Sierra. I cannot tell you how honored I am to have Kathy involved in the creation of this book. Kathy delighted me when she agreed to write the foreword. I was hoping she would because she's had such an impact on my thoughts and ideas on how brands can better connect with and empower their fans. But Kathy was also willing to review the majority of the manuscript and give me painstakingly detailed advice on how to improve it. Her advice helped me bring clarity and structure to the book. Above all, she constantly told me to ask myself on every page, "Is this helping the reader kick ass?" When the dust settled, I think I have a book that does just that—and Kathy deserves much of the credit.

Index

ABC News, Groupon story by, 119–120, 194

Advocacy, fan trust leading to, 130

Alamo Drafthouse
  Cooper's praise of CEO of, 190
  customer reactions to, 21, 29, 190
  League as CEO of, 21, 190
  movie theater policy of, 20–21, 29, 82, 190
  movie viewing experience at, 29, 82, 190
  YouTube commercial by, 190

Amazon reviews, 65

Angel Needs a Ride, 3

Apology, brand's immediate use of, 112

Apple
  customer understanding by, 81, 94, 96
  as "rock star brand," 80–81

Artist, 2

At Folsom Prison, 75–77

Autograph signing, Swift's, 184

Backstage, as customers' behind-the-scenes access, 30

"Bad Romance," 92–93

BAP. *See* Brand advisory panel

BAP chairperson, 161–162

Beebe, Susan, 136

Behind the scenes, as customers' inside access, 30

Billboard, 30

Blink-182
  fan-created videos mashup by, 72, 193
  fans rewarded for "stealing" by, 71–72
  "Up All Night" and, 71–72, 75

Bloggers, phone calls to, 73–74

Blogs
  "bigger idea behind brand" in, 65–66, 192
  CDC's successful use of, 59–60, 192
  community managers and, 44
  customer-centric, 26–27
  deletion of abusive comments on, 115
  FedEx's response to damaged goods delivery on, 194
  Fiskars' hands-off approach in, 39, 41, 47–48
  Graco's strategy for, 19–20, 24, 47
  Groupon's response to Super Bowl ads on, 194
  HomeGoods' focus on decoration in, 52–53
  ownership of, 39, 41, 42–43
  participation in, 27–28
  Patagonia's, 56, 192
  selling the benefit in, 51–53
  target audience understanding in, 27–28
  writers of, 19

Board Reader, 18, 190

Brains on Fire, Fiskars and, 37–38, 191

Brand advisory panel (BAP)
  brand ambassador program and, 160,
    173
  as brand's voice, 160–161
  CAP and, 173
  customer compensation for, 165
  customer feedback distribution and,
    160
  customer insights and, 173
  functions of, 159–160, 161
  insight drawing and, 173
  positive impact of customer
    connection and, 166–167
Brand advocacy, as priority of marketing,
  xv
Brand ambassador program
  ambassador empowerment crucial in,
    156–157
  BAP and, 160, 173
  CAP and, 163–164
  company losing control in, 153
  customer contact and, 174–175
  leadership council and, 157
  Maker's Mark and, 149, 150–152,
    153–154
  meeting frequency of, 178
  objectives, determination of, 153
  participant selection in, 154
  participants treated as employees in,
    156
  size of, 151, 155, 178
  special customers chosen in, 148
  YouTube's, 148
Brand ambassadors
  actionable insights from, 178
  "backstage pass" as compensation for,
    155–156, 165
  CAP guidelines for, 174–175
  empowerment of, 153, 157
  as feedback collectors, 175–176
  as information providers, 177
  insights to leadership council by, 178
  sales and, 177
  selection criteria for, 138, 155
Brand attributes, 140–141
Brand liaison, 163, 164
Brand loyalty
  Loyalty Graph and, 5–6
  rock star marketing and, 7–8

Brand manager, 142
Brand marketing, 4–5
Brand voice consistency, employee
    training in, 138
Brands
  advisory panel for, 44
  bigger idea behind, 65–66
  blogger contact and, 73–74
  compelling content and, 50–51
  connection with superfans by, 138
  cost savings for, 91
  customer appreciation by, 185
  customer conversations, participation
    in by, 129
  customer feedback about, 130–131
  customers at arm's length and, 31
  customers converted to fans by, xvi,
    63, 133
  delight of existing fans and, 171–172
  detractors and, 113–115
  fan cultivation for selling of, xvi–xvii,
    80, 84–85
  fan education about features of, 90
  fan list for, 22
  fans' best interests and, 106, 186
  as fans' voice, 187
  Fiskateers' sense of ownership and,
    40
  focus on problem solving by, 51–52
  formal fan connection process for,
    127–128
  friendly online tone of, 108–109
  goals of, 180–182
  good social skills reflect positively on,
    176–177
  "human voice" and, 118–119
  measurement of social media effec-
    tiveness by, xv
  negative feedback and, 122–123
  online monitoring of, 18–19, 135
  product-oriented details about, 63
  "rock star," xvi, 80–81
  rock stars and, 4–5, 10, 84
  rules for criticism response by,
    109–111, 116
  understanding fans' love of, 89, 93,
    95, 96
  word-of-mouth marketing and, 31
Burtt, Alison, 116

CAP. *See* Customer advisory panel
CAP chairperson, 164
CAP liaison, 163
Cash, Johnny
    fan connection in small groups by, 171
    At Folsom Prison and, 75–77
    "Folsom Prison Blues," 76, 77
Centers for Disease Control (CDC),
        Zombie Apocalypse blog post by,
        59–60, 192
Chatter, 146
Chief marketing officers (CMO), IBM
        survey of, xiv–xv, 189
Churn rate, brand loyalty and, 7
The Cleanest Line, as Patagonia's blog,
        56, 192
CMA Music Festival, 184
CMO. *See* Chief marketing officers
CNET, coverage of Nestlé on Facebook
        by, 195
Communication
    advisory panels and, 159–161
    employee social media tools and,
        145–146
    social media's impact on, 45–46
    two-way, 130
Compensation
    brand ambassadors and, 155–156, 165
    customers on panels and, 165
Competition, fans' feedback on, 91
Competitive advantage, teaching
        customers and, 54, 64
Competitors, customer conversations
        and, 141
Complaints, 111, 112, 113
Concerts
    artist's marketing by, 1
    Cash and, 75–77
    Jewel and, 2–3, 4
Cooper, Anderson, 190
Copyright infringement, 72
Criticism, online response to, 107–111, 116
Critics. *See* Detractors
Crowdsourcing
    pros and cons of, 92
    Super Bowl commercials and, 31
Customer advisory panel (CAP)
    brand ambassador guidelines from,
        173–175

Dell Computer and, 23
Fiskars and, 165–166
functions of, 159–160, 161
member compensation for, 165
member selection and, 168–170
positive impact of, 166–167
Customer appreciation
    brand and, 185
    as existing behavior reward, 22, 69–71,
        73
    for negative feedback, 110
Customer communication, 10
    fans coached about, 91
    polite tone in, 114, 122–123
    skills in, 169–170
Customer communication officer, 164
Customer conversations
    brand attributes and, 140–141
    brands' participation in, 129
    competitors and, 141
    evaluation of, 132
    insight drawing from, 139–140
    new opportunities and, 141
Customer feedback
    1993 status of, xiii
    BAP and, 160
    customer advisory panel and, 160–161
    distribution of, 133, 141–142, 160
    process for, 130–131
    research of, 25
Customer feedback distribution, BAP
        and, 160
Customer insights, BAP and, 173
Customer reactions, Alamo Drafthouse
        and, 21, 29, 190
Customer understanding
    Apple and, 81, 94, 96
    brands and, 22, 24, 27, 65–66
    core problem solution and, 26
    Fiskars and, 38–39
Customers. *See also* Fans
    acquiring of, 7–8
    analysis of, 57
    Apple addressing future wants of, 81
    appreciation of, 22, 69–71, 185
    behind-the-scenes contact and, 30
    blog ownership by, 39, 41, 42–43
    as brand advisory panel members, 159,
        160, 161, 163, 164

brand ambassador program and, 150–152, 154–155, 175
companies and, 3
core problems of, 26
cultivating relationship with, 80
culturing of, 6
dialogue with, 22–23
direct interaction with, 179
experience improvement of, 23
fans and, 7–8
feedback research on, 25
Graco's, 24
interaction with, 29–30
Jobs and, 81
King Arthur Flour blog content and, 58
loyalty and, xv, 54–55
marketing through connecting with, 63, 82
negative feedback from, 107–108, 113
offline communications with, 24–25, 66
online conversations of, 18–19
Red Bull's inspiration of, 64–65
respectful of, 110
rock stars and, 4–5, 10, 84
trust cultivation of, 16–17
Customers serving on panels, compensation of, 165

The Dark Knight, Warner Bros. promotion of, 28–29, 191
Deadheads, as Grateful Dead fans, 39
Dell CAP event, 156
Dell Computer, 93
consistent online voice of, 138–139
Customer Advisory Panel at, 23
decline in negative feedback for, 107–108
Dell CAP event and, 156
IdeaStorm's use by, 144–145
Dell Customer Advisory Panel
Dell and, 23
Dell's LinkedIn Group for, 23
fans' love of Dell brand and, 93
Detractors
conversion of, 108–111, 113, 122–123
dealing with, 113–115
deleting abusive comments of, 115
encouraging further feedback from, 111
four types of, 113–114

Hardwood Artisans and, 116–117, 119, 194
identification of, 113
listening to, 109
Disclosures, 104
Disney, 165
The Donnas
fan encouragement by, 75
thedonnasmedia.com and, 32–33, 191
Thedonnasmedia.com, 32–33, 191
Dropbox, 145

EDA. See Everyday Angels
E-mail
"bigger idea behind" brand in, 66
blogger interview by, 74–75
brand ambassador feedback by, 178
employee communication and, 147
fan relationship building with, 4, 23
Jewel's use of, 2, 4
Employee collaboration tools, 143–144, 145
Employee communication, 145–146
Employee training
brand voice consistency and, 138
social media marketing and, 134
Employees
as brand advisory panel members, 159, 160, 161, 162, 164
as customers, 17, 29
e-mail communication by, 147
Engineers Without Borders (EWB), 48
Environment, Patagonia and, 56
Everyday Angels
Angel Needs a Ride and, 3
as hardcore fans, 39
Jewel's free concert for, 2–3, 4
EWB. See Engineers Without Borders

Facebook
brand content study by, 50–51, 191
fan relationship building with, 23
King Arthur Flour and, 58
MarketingProfs' private group on, 145–146
Nestlé attacked by Greenpeace on, 121–122, 195
Red Bull's non-product focus on, 62–63, 193

Fan connection process, brands' lack of, 128

Fan connections, xvii

Fan insights and collaboration officer, 162

Fan trust, 130

Fan-centric brand, 127–128

Fans
active promoters sublist among, 35
advantages of marketing through, 7
as ambassador candidates, 154–155
Apple's understanding of, 81, 94, 96
appreciation of, 22, 70–71, 73, 74, 75, 79
as best marketers, 82–83
book written for, 186
brand advocates and, 80
brand knowledge also desired by, 63
brand promotion by, 90
Cash's prison concert for, 75–77
characteristics of, 7
common thread of, 94
connection with, 35–36, 166, 169, 171
contact person for, 36
contact with, 22–23, 36
control shift to, 46, 72
cultivation of, xvi–xvii, 11–12, 80, 84–85
customer communication coaching of, 91
customer conversion to, xvi, 63, 133
empowerment of, 74–75, 135, 138, 172
engaging with, 37
Everyday Angels as, 3–4, 39
as feedback channel, 91
identification of, 11–12, 22, 172
Jewel's free concert for, 2–3, 4
Lady Gaga's appreciation of, 68, 69
list of, 22, 35
main desire of, 186
monitoring of, 74
Palmer's means of connecting with, 10
as partners, 31
positive impact of connecting with, 166–167
power of personal contact with, 185–186
product preferences of, 94
profile of, 97–98
project ownership of, 4
pros and cons of, 98–99

as the real rock stars, 187
referral tools of, 105
relations with, 106
resolution of customer issues by, 90–91
rock star promotion by, 33, 83–84
rock stars as, 15, 81–82
rock stars' desire to connect with, xiv, 24
rock stars' emotional connection with, 3, 15, 80, 83–84
rock stars give ownership to, 67–68
sales through cultivation of, 80, 84–85
social media marketing goals and, 180–182
as source of marketing content, 92
spotlight on, 34–37
Swift's T-Party for, 78–79
trust cultivation of, 16–17
understanding of, 22, 24, 89, 92, 95, 96

Farley, Jim, as Ford's CMO, 102–103

FedEx, damaged goods YouTube video and, 111–112, 116, 193, 194

Feedback loop, as linkage of internal and external conversations, 178–179

"Firework," video contest promotion for, 34–35, 37

Fiskars
blog successes at, 39, 41, 47–48
Brains on Fire and, 37–38, 191
CAP and, 165–166
customer research by, 38–39
fans' marketing effectiveness for, 82–83, 191
marketing and, 185, 191

Fiskateers
exclusivity of, 40
ownership of, 41
passion sharing and, 55–56
sales impact of, 41, 55, 191
as scrapbookers, 39–40

Folsom Prison, Cash's concert at, 75–77

"Folsom Prison Blues"
as country Single of the Year for 1968, 77
as prison inmate anthem, 76

Ford
customer contact by, 183, 186
Farley as CMO of, 102–103
Monty as social media head for, 183

outreach campaign at, 102–103
social media's advertising cost
reduction for, 102
Fortune 500 companies, xv–xvi
Fun
CDC's use of, 60
Warner Bros.' use of, 28–29
Fundraising, Palmer's Kickstarter project
and, 9, 10, 190

Get Glue, 8
Google, 42
Google Alerts, 135
Google Blog Search,
18, 190
Graco
blog strategy of, 19–20, 24, 47
blog writers for, 19
customer understanding by, 24
customer-centric marketing material
by, 82
marketing and, 185
Grammy nomination, 50
The Grateful Dead, 39
Greenpeace, Nestlé and, 121–122, 195
Greubel, David, 15–16
Griffin, Patti, 3
Groupon
2011 Super Bowl commercials of, 119
ABC News article about, 119–120, 194
backlash to commercials of, 120–121
New York Times article about, 120, 194
response to Super Bowl ads backlash
by, 194

Hamel, P. J.
as King Arthur Flour employee, 57–58
video interview with, 192
Handley, Ann, 145
Hardwood Artisans
conversion of detractors by, 116–117,
119, 194
fans' support of, 117, 119
Harley-Davidson
employees as customers of, 17, 29
social media and, 17–18
HomeGoods
blog focus on decoration by, 52–53
Openhouse blog of, 52–53, 192

HootSuite, 118
Huang, Gloria, 118

IBM's CMO survey, top marketing
priorities and, xiv–xv, 189
IdeaStorm, 144–145
Influencer outreach campaign
goal of, 100–101
participant selection in, 99–100
participant treatment in, 105–106
participants' communication in, 105
timely answers to questions in, 103–104
Influencers
connection with, 166, 169
creation of custom tweets for, 104
Disney and, 165
ongoing responsiveness to, 105–106
profile of, 97–98
pros and cons of, 98–99
subject matter experts and, 136–137
Walmart and, 165
Insight drawing
BAP and, 173
customer conversations and, 139–140
Instant messaging, 146
Internet access, 1993 status of, xiii

Jewel
Angel Needs a Ride and, 3
fans' e-mail list and, 2, 4
JewelStock fan concert and, 2–3, 4, 189
Jobs, Steve, 81
Jumbotron, 68
"Just Do It," Nike and, 61

Kickstarter, 9, 10, 190
King Arthur Flour
basic questions asked by, 58
Facebook customer focus group for, 58
Hamel as employee of, 57–58
video interview with Hamel of, 192
Kit Kat, Greenpeace's attack on Nestlé
and, 121–122
Klout and Kred, 96

Lady Gaga
appreciation of fans by, 69
fan food from, 68
fan message of, 67

Little Monsters and, 68
  "Marry the Night" and, 69
Leadership council
  brand ambassador program and, 157
  function of, 178
League, Tim
  as Alamo Drafthouse CEO, 21
  CNN journalist's praise of, 190
  customer reactions to, 21, 29
  movie theater policy of, 21, 29, 82
Legal issues, 108
"Letters from the Field," 48
LinkedIn, 23
Little Monsters
  Lady Gaga's fans as, 68
  origin of, 92–93
Loyalty Graph, brand loyalty and, 5–6
Loyalty program
  fan appreciation and, 70–71
  punch cards as, 71

Maker's Mark
  ambassador stickers from, 90
  brand ambassador program of, 149,
    150–152, 153–154
  Wall Street Journal article and, 149, 195
Marketing
  basic questions in, 57
  "bigger idea behind" content in, 50–51
  brand advocacy as priority of, xv
  brand ambassador empowerment in,
    153, 157
  brand ambassador program size and,
    151
  brand ambassadors' focus in, 174–175
  brand contacting bloggers directly as,
    73–74
  brand cultivating advocates and, 80
  brand's delight of existing fans as,
    171–172
  common fan thread in, 94
  customer connection as, 82
  customer loyalty as priority of, xv
  customer-centric, 63, 82
  customers as adepts in, 45
  customer's core problems and, 26
  The Donnas' fan-run site and, 32–33, 191
  emotional connection and, 80
  existing behavior rewards in, 69–71

fan appreciation as, 73
fan connections as focus of, xvii
fan control in, 72, 75, 82–83
fans' active participation in, 36
fans and, 82–83
Fiskars' success in, 41, 185, 191
focus on problem solving in, 51–52
fun promotional activities in, 28–29
goal adjustment in, 182
Graco and, 185
King Arthur Flour's basic questions
  in, 58
knowledge of fans and, 95, 96
Maker's Mark ambassadors and, 150
McLachlan's use of "bigger idea" in, 50
Nike's celebration of active lifestyles
  and, 61
Patagonia's customer focus in, 56, 192
personal connections and, 184–185
product-oriented details in, 63
"push" model of, 45
Red Bull's focus on athletes in, 62–63, 83
Red Bull's inspiration of customers
  and, 64–65
Samuels' personal customer relationships and, 150
selling the benefit in, 26, 47, 51–53
social media tools and, xvii
Swift's T-Party and, 78–79
trust's role in, 33
Twitter engagement impact in, 101
value proposition creation in, 26
video promotions alternatives in, 34
word-of-mouth, 31
YouTube's ambassadors program and,
  148–149
Marketing priorities, 2011 IBM survey
  and, xiv–xv, 189
MarketingProfs
  private Facebook group of, 145–146
  as a virtual company, 145
"Marry the Night," 69
Mashable, 29–30
Mason, Andrew
  Groupon Super Bowl commercials
    and, 120–121
  New York Times article and, 120, 194
McBride, Terry, as Nettwerk's CEO,
  16–17

McLachlan, Sarah
  Grammy nomination for, 50
  "World on Fire" video content by, 49–50
  "World on Fire" video production by,
    48–49
Miami Vice, 73–74
Moleskine
  blog logo contest of, 43
  contest failures of, 43–44
Monster Ball tour, 68, 92–93
Monty, Scott, Ford and, 183
Morse, Katie, Billboard and, 30
Movie theater annoyances, 20
Movie theater policy, League and, 20–21,
  29, 190
Mulally, Alan
  as CEO of Ford, 183
  customer contact by, 183

Negative feedback
  appreciation of, 110
  brands' control of outcome and,
    122–123
  deletion of, 114–115, 122
  Dell's online decline in, 107–108
  FedEx's response to, 111–112, 116, 193
  Groupon's 2011 Super Bowl commer-
    cials and, 119–120, 194
  Hardwood Artisans' response to,
    116–117, 194
  high value on, 176
  interaction with customers and,
    107–108, 113
  rules for online response to, 107–111
Nestlé
  Crisis situation on Facebook page of,
    121–122, 195
  Kit Kat as criticized product of, 121
Nettwerk
  legal defense of music fan by, 16–17
  McBride as CEO of, 16–17
New York Times, Groupon story in, 120,
  194
Nike, marketing campaign of, 61

Offline customer contact
  "bigger idea behind" brand in, 66
  customer understanding through,
    24–25

Ogilvy PR, 102–103
Online conversations
  brand monitoring in, 18–19, 135
  customer interactions in, 29–30
  fan monitoring in, 74
  friendly tone in, 108–109
  Google Alerts and, 135
  Graco's participation in, 24
  negative feedback response in, 107–111
  Radian6 and, 135
  three sides of, 108–109
Online forums, 155
Online search engine
  Board Reader as, 18, 190
  Google as, 42
  Google Blog Search as, 18, 190
Openhouse blog, HomeGoods and,
  52–53, 192
Outdoors, Patagonia's focus on, 56
Outreach candidates
  interest level of, 101
  list of, 101
  relevant pitch to, 102, 103
  responsiveness to, 103–104
Overton, Melody, Starbucks and, 93–94,
  193

Palmer, Amanda
  fan connection in small groups by, 171
  Get Glue and, 8
  Kickstarter fundraising and, 9, 10, 190
  secret fan show by, 8–9
Patagonia
  The Cleanest Line blog of, 56, 192
  customer themes focus by, 56
Perry, Katy
  "Firework" video contest of, 34–35, 37
  marketing through fans and, 82
Pew Internet, smartphone user statistics
  of, 123, 195
Pitney Bowes
  24-hour response policy of, 42
  User Forum of, 42, 191
Products
  analysis of, 57
  "bigger idea behind," 47–48, 83
  selling the benefit of, 26, 51–53
  value creation through teaching and,
    54

Punch cards, as loyalty program, 71
"Push" model of messaging, 45

QR codes, *xvi*
Quinn, Mike
    Engineers Without Borders and, 48
    "Letters from the Field" and, 48

Radian6, 135
Recording Industry Association of
    America (RIAA), 15–16
Red Bull
    branding path of, 61–63
    customers inspired by, 64–65
    Facebook page of, 193
    focus on athletes by, 62–63
    non-product marketing focus of, 83
    target market of, 62
    YouTube channel of, 192
Red Cross
    "human voice" of, 118–119
    response to potential Twitter crisis by,
        118–119
Referrals, fans' tools for, 104–105
Response, quick, 109
RIAA. *See* Recording Industry Associ-
    ation of America
Rock star brand, Apple as, 80–81
Rock stars
    1993 career path of, xiv
    "bigger idea behind" music and,
        47–48
    brands and, 4–5, 10, 84
    characteristics of, 12
    fan appreciation by, 68, 69, 79, 185
    fan base growth for, 33
    fan connection desired by, 24
    fan control and, 31
    fan control of marketing by, 7, 8,
        82–83
    fan message of, 67
    fan ownership encouraged by, 67–68
    as fans, 15, 81–82
    fans and, xiv
    fans' emotional connection to, 3, 15,
        80, 83–84
    fans' promotion of, 33, 83–84
    live performances and, xiii
    sales as objective of, 84

sales through fan cultivation by, 80,
    84–85
small intimate fan groups and, 171
"Rogue tweet," 118
ROI, social media marketing goals and,
    179–181

Sales
    brand advocates' driving of, 80
    brand ambassadors' referral of, 177
    fan cultivation as basis of, 80, 84–85
    Fiskateers' impact on, 41, 55, 191
    rock stars' objective as, 84
Samuels, Bill, 150
Scissors, Fiskars and, 38–39
Scrapbookers
    Fiskars and, 38–39
    Fiskars' blog controlled by, 39
    as Fiskateers, 39–40
Skype, 145
Smartphone statistics, Pew Internet
    report on, 123, 195
SME. *See* Subject matter expert
Social Butterfly Guy, King Arthur Flour
    and, 57–58, 192
Social media
    Apple and, 80–81
    business success and, 123
    comment deletion in, 114–115, 122
    communication efficiency of, 45–46
    community managers and, 44
    compelling content on, 50–51
    content focus on customer in, 57
    customer communication through, 10
    customer responses research in, 25
    fan cultivation through use of,
        xvi–xvii, 11–12
    fan monitoring in, 74
    fans' marketing content and, xv
    Ford's advertising cost reduction
        through, 102
    Hardwood Artisans' detractors and,
        116–117, 119, 194
    Harley-Davidson's customers and,
        17–18
    inaccurate information correction in,
        110–111, 113–114
    marketing dollars shifting to, xv
    Palmer's use of, 10

potential crisis situation in, 119
selling the benefit in, 51–53
Thornton's response applauded on, 112, 116
Social Media Examiner, 29
Social media marketing goals
adjustment of, 182
brand's definition of, 180–182
prioritization of, 182
ROI and, 179–181
Social media marketing program, 181–182
Social media marketing team
decentralized "spokes" and, 134
establishment of, 133–134
fan feedback tracking by, 134–135
fan-centric brand and, 133
feedback loops between, 178–179
goal of closer fan connection and, 135–136
tagging by, 137
Social media tools
constant evolution of, xvii
customer complaint routing with, 144
employee collaboration through, 143–144
employee morale improvement through, 145–146
employees' questions answered with, 144
IdeaStorm and, 144–145
MarketingProfs and, 145
Social networking sites, 147
Sponsorships, Red Bull and, 62
Starbucks, 93–94, 193
Starbucks Melody, 93–94, 193
Subject matter expert (SME)
brand identification of, 113, 115
influencers and, 136–137
Super Bowl
commercials for, 31
Groupon's commercials for, 119–120, 194
Superfans
as brand ambassadors, 155
identification of, 138
Sustainability, Patagonia and, 56
Swift, Taylor
autobiographical songs of, 83

CMA Music Festival autograph signing by, 184
fan connection in small groups by, 171, 172
fan T-Party of, 78–79

Tagging
brand, 136
content, 135–136
influencer, 136–137
social media marketing team and, 137
Teaching
competitive advantage and, 54
content sharing and, 55, 64
customer loyalty through, 54–55
passion sharing and, 55–56, 64–65
product use and, 54, 64
Technology
1993 status of, xiii
rock stars' use of, xiv
Thilk, Chris, Miami Vice blog post by, 73–74
Thornton, Matthew, FedEx and, 112, 116
T-Party, Swift's marketing through, 78–79
Trial and error, marketing goals adjustment by, 182
Trust, marketing and, 129–130
TV commercials, Red Bull's, 62–63
Twitter
CDC's Emergency account on, 59–60, 192
engagement impact of, 101
Lady Gaga's promotion through, 69
Red Cross' potential crisis on, 118–119
response efficiency of, 45–46

Universal, Miami Vice and, 73–74
"Up All Night," Blink-182 and, 71–72, 75
User Forum, Pitney Bowes and, 42, 191

Waldow, D. J., Social Butterfly Guy and, 57–58, 192
Wall Street Journal, Maker's Mark and, 149, 195
Walmart, social media influencers and, 165
Warner Bros., The Dark Knight movie promotion by, 28–29, 191

Washington Post, Hardwood Artisans business review in, 116–117, 194

Website analytics, sales tracking through, 177

Wiki, 147, 178

Wilkins, Kaitlyn, Ford outreach campaign and, 102–103, 186

Work-flow system, customer feedback distribution and, 142

"World on Fire" music video
  "bigger idea behind," 50
  charitable giveaway of budget for, 49
  content of, 49–50
  Grammy nomination for, 50
  McLachlan's production of, 48–49
  thematic connection of audience with, 50

X Games, 61–62

Yaa, Christy, 48, 50

Yammer, 146

YouTube
  Alamo Drafthouse commercial on, 190
  as ambassador program marketing tool, 148
  Blink-182's promotion on, 72, 193
  brands' marketing with, 148–149
  FedEx damaged goods delivery on, 111–112, 116, 193
  Red Bull and, 62, 192

Zombie Apocalypse, CDC natural disaster preparation and, 59–60, 192